Hudson Taylor

God's Adventurer

Phyllis Thompson

D1125255

OMF BOOKS

Published by OMF International
10 West Dry Creek Circle, Littleton CO 80120

ISBN : 978-1-929122-03-3

First published 1954
This printing 2014

OMF BOOKS

OMF Books are distributed worldwide.
Visit *www.OMFBooks.com* for more information.

CONTENTS

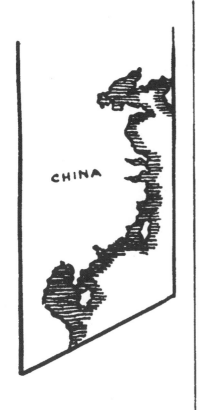

"Go for me to China."

1
"FLAT BROKE"

It was after ten o'clock on a dark night, and the shabbily dressed man accompanying him was a complete stranger. Nineteen-year-old Hudson Taylor fingered his one remaining half-crown[1] to make sure it was still in his pocket, and looked around him rather apprehensively. A half-crown in those days was about a day's wage for most people. He had been along these poor, narrow streets before, and even in broad daylight they were not attractive.

Now, with street lamps flickering feebly at the corners of dark alleys, and suspicious-looking people slinking into doorways, the neighborhood looked anything but safe and respectable. It was certainly not the sort of place one would choose to walk in with strangers after dark. But, after all, if he was going to China he must no doubt get used to this sort of thing, so he went on.

"Why didn't you ask a priest to come and pray with your wife?" he asked his companion, rather glad to hear the familiar sound of his own voice. The man had come to him with the story that his wife was dying. "Will you come and pray for her soul?" he had requested, and Hudson Taylor had agreed. Now, however, he was beginning to wonder. The man was evidently a Roman Catholic. If his wife were indeed dying, why had he not sent for a priest, of whom there always seemed to be plenty in this Irish quarter of Hull? Why come to a Protestant?

1 Eight half-crowns made a pound, in days when a pound would buy what 20 pounds will buy now.

The man explained. He had been to the priest. The priest, however, had demanded half a day's earnings down before he would help. Since he and his family were starving already, and had no money left at all, such a big fee for a prayer was quite out of the question.

Starving! Hudson fingered the coin in his pocket uneasily. It was all he had. Apart from two bowls of porridge in his boarding house, he had no other food nor money. He could hardly be expected to part with that one remaining coin. He felt unreasonably annoyed with the man, and told him what he thought of him for having got himself into such difficulties. Why had he not gone to the Relief Officer and asked for help? A dying wife and starving family, and doing nothing about it, indeed!

"I went," replied the man dismally. "He told me to come back tomorrow morning at eleven. But my wife, she be dying. She'll be gone before morning, I'm afraid."

Hudson's heart was touched. His own position had seemed precarious enough, but how much worse off was this man. If only his half-crown were in two or three pieces so that he could divide it, he thought to himself, how gladly would he have given him one of his coins.

The man turned suddenly out of the street, and into a dark courtyard. Hudson had been here before, and he remembered the last occasion very distinctly. He had been pushed and punched by the indignant slum dwellers who had torn up the tracts he gave them, and told him to get out. If he showed his face here again, he would know what was coming to him! The priest with his crucifix and prayers to Holy Mary was welcome enough, but not a young English Protestant preacher.

Hudson had departed with what dignity he could muster, doubting he would ever be invited to return. As he felt his way gingerly up a rickety flight of stairs in one of the tenement houses, he sincerely hoped that his presence would not become widely known. He was quite relieved when they reached the top of the stairs and he heard his companion open a door. They had reached their destination.

What a sight met his eyes! The dim light from a cheap, guttering candle revealed bare boards, a curtainless window, and a room almost devoid of furniture. On the floor in a corner, lying on a straw mattress was a thin exhausted woman, and beside her a newborn baby, not yet two days old. Four or five children in ill-fitting clothes, without shoes or socks, looked towards their father and the stranger he had brought with him with large hungry eyes.

Hudson stood silently in the room, thinking painfully about his half-crown. Oh, if only it were in three separate coins, he thought. Certainly he would immediately give two of them to these poor people. But it was no use wishing. He pulled himself together, remembered that he was a preacher and intended being a missionary, and decided he must tell these people about God.

"You know, things are very bad for you just now," he faltered. "But you mustn't be cast down. We have a Father in heaven who loves us and cares for us, if we trust him."

The words seemed to stick in his throat. "Hypocrite!" something inside him seemed to say. "Telling these people about a kind and loving Father in heaven—and not prepared to trust him yourself, without your half-crown!"

Hudson gave up trying to preach. The family looked at him in silence, as he stood there before them in his long-tailed coat and wide wing collar, wearing real leather shoes and a top hat. What if his clothes were getting threadbare, and his shoes needed mending? Compared with them, he appeared wealthy beyond their dreams. How were they to know he only had a half-crown left in the world? These thoughts depressed him. Oh, if only that half-crown could be divided up, he would give them most of it, he really would, and keep only a little for himself! But it was all in one piece and couldn't be shared.

He turned to the man, and said: "You asked me to come and pray with your wife. Let us pray now." It would be easy to pray, he thought, as he knelt on the bare floor. But it wasn't. No sooner had he started "Our Father who art in heaven," than that accusing voice within said again, ". . . that half-crown in your pocket!" He struggled through his prayer, feeling more and more miserable, and then stood up.

The man said to him in desperation, "You can see what a terrible state we're in, sir. For God's sake, help us!"

Suddenly, that settled that. Hudson immediately remembered something he had read often in the Sermon on the Mount. "Give to him that asketh thee."

Slowly he put his hand in his pocket. The half-crown—all of it—would have to go.

"You may think I'm well off," he said to the man, as he handed him the coin. "But as a matter of fact, that's all the money I've got in the world." Surprisingly, he began to feel quite cheerful. "But what I've just been telling you is true, you know. God really is a Father, and we can trust him. I can trust him. . . ." And he knew that he could.

He found himself speaking with great assurance and confidence about trusting God, simply because the half-crown was out of his pocket and in the man's hand. He was amazed at the difference it made to his feelings. He was on top of the world now.

He and the family parted from each other on the best of terms, he made his way down the rickety stairs and out into the courtyard, walking home with his head in the air, coat-tails flapping in the wind. He was singing at the top of his voice, without a care or a penny in the world! When he reached the small bed-sitting room in Drainside where he was living, and prepared to eat his second-to-last bowl of porridge, he was happy as a king.

An interesting thought occurred to him as he sat there. He remembered that he had read somewhere that "he that giveth to the poor lendeth to the Lord." It put that half-crown in a different light to feel that, having given it to some poor people, he had merely lent it to God. The idea of lending God half a crown might seem rather startling, but since it was in the Bible he knew it was all right. So when he knelt to say his prayers before going to bed, he mentioned the matter of the loan, requesting that it might be replaced soon, otherwise he would have no dinner the next day.

The following morning began as usual, and he looked at his last bowl of porridge. A hard day's work lay before him, and while one good bowl of porridge was enough to start on, it was hardly enough to continue on. When would God repay that loan?

He sat down and began to eat. He heard the postman at the front door, but paid little attention, since he rarely received letters on Mondays. Within a few seconds his land-lady appeared at his door.

"Here's a little package for you, Mr. Taylor," she said cheerfully, holding it towards him in her apron, for her hands were wet.

"Oh! Thank you!" replied Hudson, rather surprised. He took it from her, and looked at it. It was addressed to him all right but he did not recognize the writing. The postmark was blurred, so that did not help him, either. He decided to open it. Slitting open the envelope, he drew out a sheet of paper; inside was a pair of kid gloves.

"Whoever is sending me kid gloves?" he thought, mystified, as he opened them up. And then something fell out. It was very small, and it gleamed. He stooped to pick it up—it was a golden half-sovereign, as much as four days' wages.

He stared at it in amazement, looked through the paper wrapping for a letter, scanned the handwriting and the postmark for a clue as to who had sent it. All in vain. He never discovered where it came from. Nor did he really care. As far as he was concerned, it had come straight from heaven. It dawned on him that not merely had his half-crown been returned, but three more besides. Suddenly he laughed aloud.

"That's good interest!" he exclaimed jubilantly. "Ha! Ha! A half-crown invested in God's bank for twelve hours brings me four times as much! This is the bank for me!"

2
WHAT IF PRAYER DOESN'T WORK?

Drainside, Hull, where Hudson Taylor lived, was called that simply because it was beside a drain. Officially, the drain went by the name of canal, but to the people living in the rows of tiny cottages built on either side of the narrow ditch, it was just a drain. Very convenient it was, too, to the inhabitants of those cottages. By merely opening their front doors and throwing hard they could dispose of all their rubbish without giving themselves any further trouble. Dirty paper, cabbage leaves, potato peelings and rotten vegetables floated about on the water unashamed, providing admirable targets for street urchins throwing stones. If the drain stank unpleasantly and was a danger after dark to those who staggered unsteadily from the public house opposite Hudson's house, the advantage of this trashbin more than compensated for these minor defects.

To Hudson the contrast between this poverty-stricken, unattractive area and the beauties of the Yorkshire town near the Pennine range from which he had come, was sharp. How different, too, was his rundown little bed-sitting room from the comfortable home over his father's chemist shop in Market Square, Barnsley.

The warm sitting-room behind the shop, with a dresser of colored china and sparkling glass, a large bookcase and comfortable sofa and chairs, seemed a palace to the little room in which he now lived. A bed in one corner, a table and a couple of chairs were his only furniture. He was lonely, too, eating his frugal meals by himself, instead of sitting down to a well spread table with his parents and two chattering younger sisters. He enjoyed teasing those sisters, with their corkscrew curls and frilly frocks. He missed them—especially Amelia. But he had come here in order to get accustomed to loneliness and hardship, so he was determined to stick it out. It was part of his preparation for living in China.

Ever since the December evening more than a year previously, when he had heard a voice saying to him "Go for me to China" he had known that he must go. He was praying at the time when he heard that voice, and although China had not been in his thoughts at all, the command was so clear and unmistakable that he had no doubt it was from God. His determination to obey caused him to leave his congenial home at Barnsley to come and work for a doctor in Hull. A little medical knowledge and experience would be useful in a strange land, he decided, and this move to Hull was but the first step in his journey towards the Far East.

There was more to this training than gaining medical knowledge. That was a small matter compared with another question which constantly confronted him. He knew no one in China, and he was going alone. Was his faith in God strong enough for him to go to a strange land and face difficulties and dangers he had never yet experienced?

"When I get out to China," he thought, "I shall have no claim on anyone for anything. My only claim will be on God. What if my faith isn't the right sort? Supposing my prayers don't work?" The more he thought about it the more he realized that he must learn to move men through God, by prayer, before he left England.

To move men through God, by prayer. The thought gripped him. Could it be done? Hudson wanted to find out. In a very simple, natural way, the opportunity to try it out

14

was presented to him through his employer.

Dr. Robert Hardey was a friendly, kind-hearted, vigorous man with a never-failing fund of good humor. It was said he made people laugh so much they were cured of half their ailments without any medicines at all! With a large practice and many claims on his time, he was too busy to attend much to business details, and one day he said to his young assistant, "Taylor, please do remind me when it is time for me to pay you your salary. I'm so busy, I'm quite likely to forget . . ."

He did forget. The time came when he was due to pay Hudson, and nothing was said. A day or two passed, and still no reference was made to the matter of his salary. Hudson was faced with two alternatives. He could ask the doctor for the money, or he could ask God. Knowing that when he got to China he would have no one to ask but God, he decided to ask him now. That was why he was down to his last half-crown on the Sunday night when he gave it away to the starving family. No wonder that when the golden half-sovereign fell out of the mysterious packet the very next morning, he laughed aloud for joy!

This was an adventure. He'd taken a risk to find out whether it worked, this idea of trusting God, and it had worked! Right in the nick of time the money had come, and God alone knew who sent it. Hudson certainly did not. All he knew was that he had not gone without a single meal through trusting God, although it looked very much as though he might. As he ate his last bowl of porridge, he felt like Elijah when the ravens arrived with dinner.

"It works! It works!" Hudson set out from home, golden half-sovereign in pocket, light-hearted and jubilant. Trusting God worked. Obeying God worked. It was a wonderful life, stimulating, exciting! Hudson might have been walking on air, he was so happy.

However, he realized that half a sovereign would not last

for ever. The main problem still remained—the payment of his salary. The cheerful, busy doctor might go on for months without remembering it, and the question was, would God remind him?

Daily Hudson prayed that the doctor might remember, and then went about his work and study, confident that something would happen. A week passed, and his money was disappearing steadily. Payment for his rent made quite a hole, but he had enough to last him until Saturday.

Saturday came. The doctor said nothing. The day wore on with a heavy slowness, until by five o'clock all the patients had been attended to, and the doctor came into the dispensary and sat, while Hudson was boiling up some medicine. Evidently he had no thought of the salary, and Hudson, carefully watching the mixture in the pan, made no reference to it. Then, quite suddenly, the doctor said: "By the by, Taylor, isn't your salary due again?"

Hudson gasped. After all, it was all right! Once more, when down to his last coin, the necessary money was coming! He gulped once or twice before replying quietly: "Yes, as a matter of fact, it was due two or three weeks ago."

"Oh, I am so sorry!" exclaimed the doctor. "Why didn't you remind me? You know how busy I am. I do wish I had thought of it a little sooner, for I sent all the money I had to the bank only this afternoon. Otherwise I would pay you at once."

Poor Hudson. The sudden dashing of his hopes was almost too much. It was as though a bucket of icy cold water had been thrown over him.

Fortunately, the concoction in the pan he was watching boiled up, and he rushed with it from the room, glad for an excuse to get away. Once alone, he threw himself on his knees. His disappointment was so great he could scarcely pray coherently. What his prayer lacked in coherence, however, it made up for in earnestness, and after a while he calmed down. Somewhat to his surprise, he found himself feeling quite cheerful again. God would certainly work for him, he thought hopefully, and although he had no money at all to pay his landlady the rent, even that knowledge did not unduly depress him.

It was late when he prepared to leave the dispensary that evening. The hands of the clock had ticked slowly round until they stood at about ten minutes to ten when he started to put on his overcoat.

"Well, my landlady will be in bed by the time I get back," he thought. "So I won't have to see her this evening and tell her I can't pay the rent this week." He walked over to the gas bracket, preparing to turn it off, when he heard the sound of footsteps outside. It was the doctor, and he was laughing heartily, as though greatly amused.

"Why, hello, Taylor, are you still here?" he exclaimed. "What do you think? One of my patients has just come round to pay his bill! He's one of the richest patients I've got, and he could have paid me by check any time. Yet here he is, bringing the money round at ten o'clock on a Saturday night!"

Hudson laughed. That a man rolling in money should come round himself to pay his doctor's bill at such a time was certainly unusual. What had possessed him? People were not usually so careful about paying doctors' bills.

The doctor made his entry in the ledger, and started back towards the door, when suddenly he turned.

"By the way, Taylor," he said. "You might as well take these notes. I have no change, but I can give you the balance of your salary next week . . . Good-night."

And Hudson, his pockets empty, was left standing in the dispensary with a handful of bank notes. His prayer was answered. Not only could he pay his landlady, not only had he money in hand for weeks ahead, but he had proved again that God answers prayer! There was no question about it now—he could go to China.

3

"YOU'RE A DEAD MAN"

Mrs. Finch, Hudson's landlady in Drainside, was married to a sailor who, as is the way with sailors, was usually at sea. His wife had a hard time making ends meet on his small allowance, and very glad she was to have the doctor's young assistant paying even a little money for the use of her front room. That was all she had to pay for the rent of the whole house, and as he gave no trouble, she considered herself very fortunate to have him. Her lodgers were not usually such respectable, considerate young gentlemen as this one, and when one day he broke the news to her that he would be leaving, she was genuinely distressed.

"I'm going to London to attend a medical course in the London Hospital," he explained.

"Well, sir, very sorry I'll be to lose you," she said. "You're going to London . . . ?" That gave her an idea.

"I wonder if you would do something for me while you are there," she asked. Certainly he would if he could. Then she explained. Half of her husband's pay was sent to her from the shipping offices in London each month, and a charge was made for sending it. If Mr. Taylor would kindly collect the money from the offices and send it to her instead, he would save her quite a lot of money.

Hudson, of course, readily agreed to do this, although once he got to London he discovered it involved a long walk in the middle of the day in order to keep his promises. Since he had a four-mile walk from his boarding-house to the hospital each morning, and a four-mile walk back each evening, he was scarcely in need of any further exercise.

This move to London to take a medical course was a big thing to him. He was already in touch with a very small mission called the Chinese Evangelization Society, which was prepared to send him to China as a missionary, and with the approval of this society he was now starting out on further medical training. It was as definite a step towards China as the move to Hull had been, and had been taken at a risk of which he spoke to no one.

The risk was again along the lines of testing his own faith, and his own ability to endure hardships. His father had offered to supply him with the money necessary to live in London and take the medical course; the Chinese Evangelization Society had made a similar offer. After thinking the matter over, however, and praying about it, too, he decided to accept neither. He thanked his father and said that he would not need his help, and his father naturally thought he was receiving his support from the missionary society. He thanked the board of the missionary society and said he would not be needing their help, and they thought he was receiving his support from his father! He arrived in London one very foggy day with the few pounds he had saved, not knowing what would happen when they were spent.

He was determined to learn to trust God to meet his needs as they arose. At the same time, he felt he must live as economically as possible. It had been arranged that he should share an attic bedroom in Soho with a cousin of his, and this he was glad to do. Far better to live with a friendly relative than be entirely alone in the great city. He bought his own food, and was very economical—he spent as little as he possibly could. After a few experiments, he decided that brown bread and apples, with clear cold water, was the most inexpensive diet he could find. So on his way to the hospital he bought a pound of apples for his dinner, and on his way back, passing warm-looking restaurants from which drifted out the most mouth-watering smells, he called in at a baker's shop and bought a brown loaf.

"Will you cut it in half, please?" he asked the baker. And with the two halves under his arm he continued his long walk home, and climbed the three flights of stairs to his room. One half of the loaf provided him with his supper, and the other half was resolutely put aside for breakfast—however hungry he felt.

"No, my health does not suffer," he wrote to reassure his mother, who was anxious about him. Was he getting proper food, she wondered? Had she known! "On the contrary, everyone says how well I look, and some even that I am getting fat!" Though this, honesty compelled him to add, "can only be perceived by rather a brilliant imagination."

About three months after his arrival in London, he received an urgent letter from Mrs. Finch. Would he, she requested, be so kind as to draw her allowance for her as soon as possible? Her rent was nearly due, and she had no other money with which to pay it.

The request had come at an awkward time for Hudson, for he was studying hard for an examination, and spent every spare minute over his books. Rather than take the time to go all the way to Cheapside, it would be better to send the money out of his own diminishing supply, and call at the shipping office to collect the remittance after he had taken the examination. This he did, little dreaming of the trouble he was getting himself into, for when eventually he went to the shipping office, the clerk told him he could not have the money. "The officer Finch has run away from his ship," he said, "and gone to the gold diggings."

"That's very inconvenient for me!" exclaimed Hudson, taken aback, "I've already advanced the money to his wife.

She'll have no means of repaying me, I know."

"I'm sorry. Very sorry indeed," said the clerk. But there was nothing he could do, of course, and Hudson departed.

After the first shock, he was not unduly worried. "After all," he thought, "I am out to trust God to provide me with what I need, as soon as my own funds are exhausted. This only brings that time nearer." As he counted up his remaining money he realized that the time was very near! The memory of his Drainside experiences encouraged him, however, and he returned to his attic feeling cheerfully confident that all would end well.

During the evening he made himself a notebook, it was cheaper than buying one. He selected some sheets of paper, fitted them together, and had started sewing them when he accidentally pricked the forefinger of his right hand. It was only a prick, and in a few seconds he had forgotten it. But that prick nearly cost him his life.

The following day at the hospital his work was to assist in dissecting the body of someone who had died of fever. It was not only an unpleasant job but a dangerous one as well. The students had been solemnly warned that the slightest scratch on their hands, should it become infected, would probably prove fatal, and they all worked carefully, avoiding anything that might damage their skin. When Hudson soon began to feel inexplicably weary, and then was suddenly sick, it did not occur to him that there was anything seriously wrong with him. He was merely surprised, since his diet was not the kind likely to cause bilious attacks! He drank a glass of cold water, felt a little better, and went to a lecture. His right arm began to ache so much that he could not write. The pain spread to his side, and he felt very ill. He could not go on like this.

"I can't think what has come over me," he said to the surgeon in the dissecting room.

"Why, what's the matter?" he inquired. Hudson tried to describe how he was feeling, and the surgeon, looking at him keenly, said, "What has happened is clear enough, I'm afraid. This is a case of malignant fever. You must have cut yourself while you were dissecting."

"No, sir, I'm sure I didn't. I haven't got a scratch or a cut."

"Well, you certainly must have had one," said the surgeon. "Let me look at your hand." While he was doing it, Hudson remembered the prick of the needle the night before. Could it be that, he asked? Yes, the surgeon thought it could.

"You'd better get home as quickly as you can," he said gravely, "and put your affairs in order." He looked at the young medical student, from whom it was useless to try to disguise the gravity of the situation.

"For," he said bluntly, "You are a dead man."

4
TOO FAR TO WALK

Hudson's first reaction to the doctor's startling pronouncement was one of sorrow and disappointment. If he were dying, that meant he could not go to China. China! How he had longed to go there. How deep had been his conviction that God had a work for him in that land. It seemed impossible that he had been mistaken about it all. Had he been mistaken? If God really intended him to go to China, thought Hudson, then he must get better, in spite of the doctor's assertion that there was no hope.

This he tried to explain. He was not afraid to die, he pointed out. The prospect of being with his Master, whom he was learning to love very much, was a very inviting one. However, he was sure he had a work to do for him in China first, and therefore he must be pulled through this illness.

"That's all very well," the doctor replied impatiently. This was no time for the young student to reason why he should live, when it was evident he was going to die. "You get home as fast as you can. You've no time to lose. You'll soon be quite incapable of winding up your affairs."

It was hardly a cheerful motive for hurrying, and, anyway, he had not enough money to pay the fare for the four-mile ride to Soho. Hudson smiled a little wryly to himself as he departed. He dragged himself slowly along the road to the place where he could get on an old horse-drawn omnibus, and wearily climbed into it, conscious of the pain in his arm as the clumsy vehicle rumbled and bumped along the streets. When he finally reached his lodging and climbed up the three flights of stairs to his attic, he was exhausted. Hoping, however, to do anything that might save his life, he cut his own finger open to let out some of the poison. The pain was intense and that was the last thing he remembered. He fell unconscious to the floor.

*   *   *   *   *

For some weeks Hudson lay in his bed, too weak to move from his room. When he had been found in a dead faint on the floor, an artist uncle of his who lived nearby had been called, and this kind man had taken charge of him, sending immediately for a doctor despite Hudson's protests that he could not afford to pay the bill.

"He is my own medical man and the bill will be sent to me," he said reassuringly. "Don't worry over that." When the doctor arrived and heard Hudson's story, he looked grave.

"Well," he said frankly. "If you've been living moderately, you may pull through. But if you've been going in for alcohol and that sort of thing, I'm afraid there's no hope."

With vivid memories of apples and brown bread washed down by cold water, Hudson was able to reassure him. If recovery depended on living simply, he knew of no one who stood a better chance.

"But now," said the doctor, "It's going to be a hard struggle. You must do everything possible to keep up your strength. A bottle of port wine every day, and as many chops as he can eat," he told Hudson's uncle. That sort of diet did not appeal to Hudson, but he did his best with it. After many days and nights of suffering he was at last able to move out of his room and lie for an hour or two on a sofa in the boarding-house lounge. It was not until then that he learned that two other medical students, who had become infected about the same time as he, were both dead. Why had his life, then, been saved? He felt it could be for no other purpose than that there was a work for him to do in China.

One day when the doctor came, after expressing satisfaction at the progress made by his patient, he said:

"The best thing you can do now is to get off to the country as soon as you feel fit to make the journey. You must rest until you have gained more strength. If you start work too soon, the result may still be serious."

When he had gone Hudson lay back on the sofa to review his position. "Get off to the country!" His thoughts flew to the cozy, happy home in Yorkshire; the Cudworth road along which he had raced so often as a child, merrily bowling his hoop and teasing Amelia as she came trotting breathlessly behind, corkscrew curls bouncing; the shady glades of the Lunn Woods, where butterflies fluttered, and birds' nests could be found; the distant view of the Pennines. "Get off to the country!" The doctor's order was wholly attractive, and commended itself to him in every way! Hudson realized that he was still far too weak to attempt the strenuous life in the hospital yet, and obviously there was nowhere he could regain his health so quickly as in his own home. There was only one obstacle in the way— he had no money at all for the fare.

Actually, as he well knew, the money could be obtained with the utmost ease just for the asking. His kind uncle would be more than willing to lend it. If he were to drop the smallest hint in a letter home, his fare and more would arrive by return of post. Yet, as he lay on the sofa, exhausted as he was after the effort of walking down the stairs, there was something in him that refused to consider taking the easy and obvious course. He still wanted to try out this method of getting used to relying on God to answer his prayers, instead of depending on those who would not be present to help him in China. He closed his eyes as he lay there and, explaining this to God, asked him what he should do.

After this prayer he remained quiet for a while, thinking over the matter. If he had not forwarded that money to Mrs. Finch, he thought, he would have had enough. If only Finch had not chosen to desert his ship at that particular time, Hudson would have been able to draw the money. Then the thought came that perhaps if he went to the shipping office he might even yet be able to draw it. It seemed unlikely, since he had forwarded the remittance to Mrs. Finch entirely on his own responsibility, but the thought persisted. Was God putting it into his mind, he wondered, or was it just a silly idea of his own? He was not sure.

He closed his eyes again and prayed, asking God which it was. If the idea did come from God, the fact remained that the shipping office was two miles away, and he had no money for a ride there. To walk in his condition was out of the question. It had been necessary for someone to help him even walk down the stairs.

Yes, to walk was out of the question—but was it? Was it? To his own surprise, Hudson found himself thinking, that perhaps it was not "out of the question," after all. God had already done some quite remarkable and unexpected things after he had prayed. Jesus Christ had said, "Whatsoever ye shall ask in my name, that will I do, that the Father may be glorified in the Son."

Jesus had said it 1,800 years before, but as Hudson lay on the boarding-house sofa, it all seemed suddenly real and up-to-date. There was something very convincing about that calm assertion. "Whatever you ask in my name, I will do it." In view of it, to walk to the shipping office in Cheapside no longer seemed out of the question. Obviously all that was necessary was to ask to be strengthened to do it. So that is what Hudson did. Then he rang for the boarding-house servant, and asked her to go up and fetch his hat and stick. Once that respectful but somewhat surprised young lady handed them to him, he slowly emerged from the house, then turned along the quiet street into the busy thoroughfare leading towards the city.

His progress, admittedly, was slow. He showed an unusual interest in the contents of shop windows, pausing at almost every other one to lean against the glass. Ladies in crinolines swept past him as he continued his deliberate, leisurely pace. Street vendors called in vain to him to buy their goods. He did not so much as turn his head to watch an elegant coach with briskly trotting horses come smartly along the street. If the young Queen Victoria herself had driven past he would not have roused himself to look.

But gradually he was making the journey. He had asked for strength to walk it, he reminded himself as he faced the sharp incline that led to Cheapside, and strength would surely be given. Walk it he did. He arrived safely at the shipping offices and sat down on the steps before attempting to climb the stairs up to the first floor. It was a little unusual, he realized, to take a seat just there. The top-hatted gentlemen who hurried past him, up and down the stairs, evidently thought so too. They eyed him with some surprise, as though thinking, "Tut, tut! Quite a respectable-looking young fellow, too." However, no one spoke to him, and eventually he reached the top and entered the office.

This was the crucial moment that brought him to this place. After all the exertion of the two-mile walk, was he to be met with a disappointment? Somehow Hudson felt it was going to be all right. And it was. The clerk who greeted him recognized him immediately.

"Oh, I am so glad you have come," he exclaimed. "It turns out that after all it was not the mate Finch who ran away, but an able seaman of the same name. I shall be glad to give you the half-pay due to Mrs. Finch up to date. It will no doubt reach her more safely through you than through her husband. His ship has just reached Gravesend, and we all know the temptations these men meet when they come ashore after a voyage." He looked keenly at the young medical student, standing so pale and obviously weak. "Before I give you the money," he continued, "you must have a rest and something to eat. I'm just going to have my lunch. You must come inside and share it with me."

Gratefully Hudson accepted the kind invitation, and he was glad of the opportunity to rest and eat. He made his journey back to Soho in an omnibus, since he could afford it now. The effort he had made seemed to have done him good rather than harm. The next morning he felt so much better that he had no hesitation about going round to the doctor's surgery to settle his bill. His uncle had already done so much for him, but Hudson was unwilling to leave him to pay it and then spend his own money on railway fares to go home for a holiday. He realized that by paying the doctor's bill himself meant he would be left with insufficient money to buy his ticket, it seemed the only honorable thing to do. So off he went to the doctor. And there a further pleasant surprise awaited him. The doctor refused to charge him anything.

You're a young medical student," he said firmly. "As such, I shall charge you nothing for my services."

"But medicines . . . ," Hudson argued. "All that quinine. I ought to pay for that."

"Very well," said the doctor. "Quinine. You can pay for the quinine, and that's all."

Hudson made a rapid mental calculation as he handed over the surprisingly small sum. When his bills were paid, there would be enough left for his railway fare to Yorkshire, the omnibus journey to his home, and the necessary food for the journey. He was overjoyed. This was wonderful. At every step he found his affairs were planned out to what seemed perfection. He simply could not keep it all to himself, this amazing evidence that God was fully prepared to take responsibility for the ordering of his life. If God did this for him, he most certainly would for others, too. The doctor must be told.

"Pardon me, sir," he said respectfully. "I wonder if you will allow me to speak to you freely, without being offended. I feel that under God I owe my life to your care and attention, and I am truly grateful. There is something I want to tell you about." He related the whole story of his reason for being in London, his intention to find out if God really answered prayer before he went to China, and the things he had experienced in doing so. The surgeon listened with kind though skeptical interest until Hudson told him of his walk to Cheapside the previous day. The doctor could not believe that.

"Impossible," he exclaimed. "Why, I left you lying on that sofa looking more like a ghost than a man!"

"I did walk it, indeed, sir," asserted Hudson, explaining that he had prayed in the name of Jesus to be strengthened to do it, before starting out.

"Do you mean you walked—you did not even go by omnibus?"

"No, I walked."

"All the way from Soho to Farringdon Street, and then up Snow Hill to Cheapside?"

"Yes, sir."

The doctor was interested now. It seemed incredible that one who had been so weakened by illness could take a two-mile walk alone through London's busy streets, and be none the worse for it. He listened to the recital of the happy outcome of the walk in the money received, how Hudson had been able to settle all his bills, and last of all, that after the price of the quinine was paid, he had just enough to see him home. There was a restrained yet evident joy about the convincing way Hudson told his story that touched the older man's heart. This practical confidence in a God who, after all, could neither be seen nor heard, was something new to him. Tears welled slowly up in his eyes as he looked at the strangely radiant expression of the open-faced boy before him. He said in a voice deepened by emotion:

"I'd give all the world for a faith like yours."

"You can have it, you know, sir," answered Hudson quietly. "It's free to all—without money and without price."

5
HOME AGAIN

The horse-drawn omnibus rattled over the cobbles, and stopped in Market Square, Barnsley. The passengers emerged one by one, and eventually Hudson appeared, tired and travel-stained after the long journey from London. How friendly and familiar everything appeared. How good it was to be welcomed back home by his strict yet genial father, bewhiskered and coat-tailed, and by his gentle mother with her smoothly brushed hair and dainty muslin cap.

How pleasant, as he walked out for a stroll, to be greeted warmly by this friend and that, glad to see him again, and eager to hear of his life in the faraway capital. It was all so different from London, where he was just an unimportant stranger, and walked along the busy streets with never a greeting from anyone to cheer him.

Weak as he still was from his illness, home was the place above all that gave him complete rest and satisfaction. He sat contentedly by the fire in the warm sitting-room behind the shop, glad of the old familiar setting that brought back so many happy memories. What scenes were revived by the sight of the large, sturdy table in the middle of the room, for instance.

Once more he was a very small boy, dressed in his best velvet suit, sitting at the table surrounded by visiting grown-ups. He was watching his mother cutting a delicious looking apple pie into generous portions, which were handed along to her guests—to everyone but her own small son, who sat politely silent, as he had been trained, waiting in vain for the plate that was intended for him. At last he realized that somehow his mother had overlooked him this time and he had been told that on no account must he ask for anything at the table! The story of his ingenuity had been told, time and time again in the family, how, during a lull in the conversation, a little voice had inquired:

"Mamma do you think apple pie is good for little boys?"

It was at the table, too, that he had sat, day after day, learning the lessons his father set for him, until eventually at the age of eleven, he went to school. Much happier he had been under his father's tuition than at school, too, though he was one of the star pupils there. There was something eminently wholesome and manly about his father, with rigid ideas of right and wrong, and unyielding discipline.

Hudson had learned to be punctual long before he had his life ruled by clanging school bells. Woe betide the one who was not ready to sit at table, hands washed and hair brushed, when it was time for a meal.

"If there are five people, and they are all kept waiting one minute, then five minutes are lost," father would say sternly, adding slowly, "Minutes that can never be found again." It was very solemn indeed.

"Learn to dress quickly," was another of his axioms. His reason, "For you have to do it once at least every day of your life." So, obviously one might as well get used to it. If Hudson smiled at these memories as he sat in the cozy home, it was with the affectionate amusement with which children think about the peculiarities of their parents. And it was interesting to remember that it was from his father he had first heard of China when, as a little five-year-old, he had heard him exclaim vehemently:

"Why don't we send missionaries there? That is the country to aim at, with its teeming population . . . strong, intelligent, scholarly people."

Now, nearly fifteen years later, Hudson himself was preparing to go there. As he spent those weeks at home, with plenty of time to think, he marveled at the way his destiny had been revealed to him. For surely this was his destiny, the particular work that was appointed for him to do? "Go for me to China." He could never forget the night when he received that divine commission.

Only one other experience, perhaps, stood out more vividly in his memory. China had not come into it, that afternoon in the old warehouse when his whole outlook on life had been completely changed, but had it not been for what took place then, certainly he would have no thought of going to China now. Many times Hudson lived through that momentous afternoon again. It was over three years ago, yet as clear in his mind as if it had happened yesterday.

He was sixteen years old, and already disappointed with life. How dull it seemed, living here at home, and helping his father in the shop. It was not that he did not love his parents, for he did, but he found their way of life boring. Balls and hunting parties found no place in their program. They preferred singing hymns in the little chapel down the road, and Hudson, dutifully accompanying them, thought it very dull indeed. He tried his best to enjoy it all as they did, but he could not. His own private desire was to live in a large house with a lot of servants, emerging splendidly in a scarlet jacket, to go hunting. He longed to be able to rush along at the greatest possible speed—on a horse, since motorcycles had not yet been invented. These daydreams, however, could never come true, and he was in a discontented mood when he wandered into the sitting room one afternoon in June, looking for something to do.

He glanced through the bookcase, but saw nothing there that appealed to him. He turned his attention to a basket of small, paper-covered books, and picked out one of them.

"I know what this will be," he thought. He knew the sort of paper-covered booklets his father collected. "It will have an interesting story to begin with, and a moral or a sermon at the end." Well, he decided, he would read the interesting story, and leave the rest. So he took it off to the warehouse across the back yard, where he would be undisturbed by younger sisters, and sat down to read it.

He little knew that at that very moment his mother, on holiday about seventy miles away, was kneeling beside her bed, praying for him with unusual earnestness and intensity. He hadn't any idea that six weeks previously his thirteen-year-old sister Amelia had determined that she would pray for him three times a day until his mind was changed about God. That was what he needed; a change of mind about God. He had told her that he was not really at all sure about God, and was very moody as a result. He was not even sure there was a God.

Not sure there was a God? Amelia, being herself quite sure about God, felt this state of affairs must not be allowed to continue. Realizing, however, that her arguments, convincing and conclusive as they appeared to her, did not seem so to him, she came to the conclusion that only God could change Hudson's mind. That is why she determined to pray three times every day, until it happened. She even made a note of her decision in her diary. For all her corkscrew curls and frilly frocks, Amelia was a young person of some determination, and pray three times a day about the matter she did.

Unaware of all this, Hudson sat in the warehouse and read the booklet. It was the reading of that little booklet that completely changed his outlook on life. Quite suddenly and unexpectedly it dawned upon him that what he had heard about God and Jesus Christ from his earliest childhood, was true. God was real. Jesus Christ was his Son, and had died for the sake of sinners. He had come to life again, and was in heaven alive, able to see everything on earth—able to see him, right there in the warehouse! He had died for the sins of the whole world; therefore he had died for the sins of Hudson Taylor. He had promised eternal life to all who believed on him—therefore he had promised eternal life to Hudson Taylor. He heard prayer, therefore he would hear Hudson Taylor's.

What a remarkable thing that, having heard it so many times before, it had only just dawned on him. Somehow, it made Hudson feel as he felt when he suddenly saw the simple solution to a mathematical problem that had puzzled him for hours — relieved, enlightened, exuberant. Everything was different now. The heavy feeling of discontent, the uneasy sensation of having done something wrong that would one day be found out, were gone. He felt free. It seemed too good to last.

But it did last. Three and a half years later, sitting contentedly by the glowing, crackling fire, Hudson knew—it lasted. The years since that afternoon had not been idle, easy ones. They had contained certain trials and hardships that were completely new to him. But there had always been the exhilarating consciousness of adventure in an unseen realm. The stimulation of finding out that God answered his prayers, that God would lead him into unexplored pathways he would never have discovered himself, was far greater than that of galloping after the hounds in the limited world of Barnsley and district. He knew the simple secret of getting rid of that sensation of guilt. He merely did what he knew to be right, and when he inadvertently did that which was wrong, he confessed it to God, who has promised to forgive when sin is acknowledged. Yes, it lasted.

The weeks at Barnsley sped past all too quickly, and

renewed in health and spirits, Hudson faced London again. But it was quite a wrench to say goodbye to home again, with its warmth and love. He was beginning to know from personal experience what it meant to tread a lonely pathway, and to go through weakness and hardship without the support of friends who thought the same way about things. But what better way to grow strong and self-reliant? Pioneer missionary work required men—not mollycoddled weaklings. Hudson, delicate from childhood, was determined to be a pioneer missionary and therefore he must be in every sense of the word, a man.

His parents, however, not unnaturally, were distinctly averse to his becoming a man if doing so involved returning to a diet of apples and brown bread washed down by water. Indeed, they had grave doubts as to whether he would ever become one that way—even Hudson himself agreed the matter was open to question. Instead of living in the Soho boarding-house and buying his own food, it was decided he should obtain a position as doctor's assistant, where he could live with the family. This he did. He attended lectures at hospital in the morning, assisted his surgeon employer from dinner-time until nine o'clock in the evening, and the rest of the day he could study for lectures.

It was a strenuous life, but he was happy. Good food and a comfortable home did make a difference to his spirits after all. During the next six months he gained not only much useful medical knowledge and experience of human nature, but further evidence of what he knew to be of even greater importance—the help God would give in all matters about which he prayed.

One outstanding example was the case of the man with gangrene. A thoroughly hardened drunkard he was, and now he lay dying, though he did not know it.

"It's no use speaking to him about religion," Hudson was

warned when he visited the home where the man lived. "He's an atheist. He won't hear a thing about religion. We asked a Scripture reader to come and visit him once, and he got in a towering rage and ordered him out of the room." The vicar of the parish had called, too. Alas, he was forced to depart in some confusion, for the infuriated invalid only permitted him to advance near enough to spit in his face.

Hudson felt like a gladiator entering the arena when he called for the first time to dress the man's foot. Speak to him about God's willingness to forgive his sins, and to receive him as the father received the prodigal, he must. The man was dying. What hope was there for him in this world or the next, without God? Hudson decided to wait a propitious occasion to broach the all-important subject. Until the angry and rebellious attitude had in some measure altered, it would be worse than useless to do so. He took special care in dressing the man's foot, and said nothing about religion for several days. But the man was on his mind. Hudson felt responsible for him, and prayed for him many times a day. "Learn to move men through God by prayer." If his prayers for the softening of hard hearts did not prove effective here in England, he could scarcely expect to be successful in China.

Gradually the man's attitude changed. It changed first of all towards Hudson. The young medical student dressed his foot so carefully and skillfully that the pain was considerably eased and he felt really grateful. He even went so far as to say so. This was the opportunity for which Hudson had waited. He explained to the man how he trusted in God to help him in all his medical work, and then went on to the subject of everyone's need of God's forgiveness and mercy.

Had he been the Scripture reader or the vicar, he would probably have fared as they did. However, as he was the doctor, and able to relieve pain, the man managed to swallow his anger, and turned his back without a word. He remained there, with his face against the wall, until Hudson departed. It was not exactly encouraging, but it was a step in the right direction. The next day Hudson broached the subject again—with the same result. After several more visits, his heart began to sink. Was it any use continuing? It seemed not. One day he felt so discouraged, so anxious about the man who, despite his ill-temper, was so often in his thoughts, that he felt something rising in his throat, and tears came to his eyes.

"Oh, friend, you must listen!" he exclaimed, and walked towards the bed. "Oh, if only you would let me pray with you!" and he found himself speaking in a broken voice, expecting the man to turn his back as usual. But the man did not. He looked with surprise at the over-wrought young doctor who was obviously so upset about something, and said:

"Well, if it will relieve you to do it, you can."

It was scarcely a warm invitation, but Hudson needed nothing more. He knelt down, closed his eyes, and prayed aloud. Oh, that God would open the eyes of the dear man! Oh, that he might know that God was real, that Jesus Christ had died to save him from the punishment due for his sins, that forgiveness was his for the asking.

The man lay silent, and although he made no comment then, it was evidently the real turning point in his life. No longer did he turn his back when Hudson spoke to him about God. The realization was dawning on him that what this earnest young man repeatedly told him was true. If it were true—why not believe it? Why not? So it came about that one day Hudson left his patient's room almost walking on air. The previously bitter, hardened old man, who had not been inside a church for forty years, and then only to get married, was lying in bed, his eyes reverently closed, learning to pray to his God.

6
ROCKS AHEAD

The ship was moving. The gangway had been removed after the friendly mate, the last man to leave the shore, had jumped aboard, and now, slowly and silently, the ship was leaving the dock-side. Hudson stood alone on deck, waving to the little group of people standing watching him depart. His eyes were fixed upon his mother. Dear, gentle, stalwart little mother. She had tried so hard to be brave, but down in his cabin, when she had been gently smoothing the bed-clothes on his bunk, he had caught her with tears on her cheeks. Now, after she had said the last goodbye and left the ship, she had sat down quickly on an old piece of timber, as though she were going to faint. Hudson had run down the gangway to her, and given her a last reassuring hug.

"Don't cry, Mother dear," he had said. "It is only for a little while. We shall meet again." But he had to hurry back on board and leave her. She was standing up now, her full skirts billowing in the breeze, waving her handkerchief to him. Hudson, hating to lose sight of her, suddenly turned and climbed up into the rigging, to get a better view. Standing there among the swaying ropes, he held on firmly with one hand, and with the other waved his hat vigorously. It would cheer her up, perhaps, to see him like that! High above his head, the sails were flapping and the masts creaking as the ship drew towards the dock gates. The beloved figure on shore seemed to be getting smaller and smaller, and her little fluttering handkerchief more minute.

"Oh-h-h!" Hudson stopped waving at the sound of that piercing cry. It was his mother. The ship was passing through the dock gates now and making for the open sea, bearing her only son away to that distant, unknown land—China. This was goodbye indeed. The anguish of that cry went through Hudson's heart like a knife. What this was costing her! She was suffering so much more than he. A lump rose in his throat.

The ship was gathering speed now, and he could no longer distinguish the little figures standing at the end of the dock. He strained his eyes, peering through the misty air until he knew he could see them no more, and slowly swung down on to the deck, the sound of that cry still ringing in his ears. A new thought was occupying his mind. If it cost his mother so much to see him leave her for China, what must it have cost God to part with His Son, when Jesus came to earth to die for man's sin? Was not God a Father? Was not Jesus "his only begotten Son"? Somehow, the sacrifice of parting that Hudson and his mother were feeling so keenly seemed to bring him nearer to God, to understand better what was meant by the love of God. God loved, so he knew what this sort of suffering was, too. Hudson felt strangely strengthened in the midst of his pain as he went down to his cabin.

He was the only passenger on the *Dumfries*, a small sailing ship of only 470 tons, and he had been told it would be five or six months before it would dock in Shanghai. In 1853 there was no Suez Canal route to the Far East, and the little ship must breast its way through the waves around the Cape of Good Hope, and brave the typhoons of the Pacific before it could reach its destination.

A long sea voyage, and one filled with enough danger and excitement during the first ten days to last him the rest of the trip. Almost as soon as the *Dumfries* entered the Irish

Channel she had to make her way in the teeth of a gale, and for days she was driven this way and that, like a cork, by the force of the winds. Hudson had never known anything like it, and rapidly revised any ideas he may have had about the romance of a sailor's life. The timbers creaked and groaned, sea water found its way into the cabins, his clothes felt damp and sticky, and as the days and nights passed, the storm seemed to increase in fury until on Sunday afternoon the seas were mountainous.

Hudson struggled up on deck, and clinging to the side of the ship, looked around on the wild scene. The sea was white now with foam, and waves came rolling, one after another, until they seemed to tower above the little *Dumfries* like threatening cliffs as it floundered in a trough of swirling water. When it seemed that it must be submerged, then the vessel would begin to tilt dangerously, and Hudson, feet sliding on the slippery deck, could scarcely keep his balance until the ship perched dizzily on top of one watery cliff only to plunge down again as the wave rushed on. As he looked across the raging seas, he saw a large ship astern, beaten along by the winds, and a little brig. How helpless they all were, and how powerless they would be if the waves dashed them together.

The captain was standing beside him, face set and anxious. Never had he seen a wilder sea, he admitted.

"Unless God helps us," he added solemnly, "there is no hope."

"How far are we from the Welsh coast?" asked Hudson. The dangerous Welsh coast with its rocks jutting out into the sea.

"Fifteen or sixteen miles." But they were drifting towards it, for the west wind was blowing. "We must carry more sail. The more sail we carry, the less we shall drift. God grant the masts can stand it!" What if they were to snap under the strain of the wind? But the risk had to be taken. Their lives were at stake. He ordered two sails to be hoisted.

The ship plunged forward, faster than ever, with the wind filling the sails. It was rolling one-sidedly, with the waves at times rushing right over the lee bulwarks. The evening was drawing on, and the sun was sinking behind a bank of clouds. Hudson watched it solemnly.

"Tomorrow thou wilt rise as usual," he thought, feeling rather dramatic. "But unless a miracle happens, all that will be left of us will be a few broken timbers floating on the waves." How his family would sorrow if he were drowned. What a waste of money for the Chinese Evangelization Society, who had spent about £100 on his outfit and passage. What would it feel like, that struggle in the raging waters before they finally closed over his head? It was a melancholy thought. Hudson felt cold and lonely and rather frightened in the gathering darkness, with the wind roaring and the spray beating into his face. He fumbled his way slowly to the gangway and descended into his cabin. Finding his hymnbook and Bible, he sat on his bunk and started to read.

"Let not your heart be troubled; ye believe in God, believe also in me." There was such a calmness about the familiar words, that somehow he began to feel calmer himself. He read on, and after a while, his eyes tired with reading in the uncertain light of the swaying lantern, he threw himself on the bunk and fell asleep.

When he awoke, it was approaching midnight. The ship was still pitching violently, and the wind roaring. How far were they now from land, and those treacherous rocks? Hudson went up on deck again. Peering across the moonlit waters, he saw a light ahead. It was the Holyhead lighthouse, sending out its warning to all ships that might be approaching too near. The Holyhead lighthouse—and the rocks.

"Can we clear it?" he shouted to the captain, the sound of his voice almost carried away by the wind.

"If we make no leeway we may just do it," the captain shouted back. "But if we drift, God help us.

They did drift. Helplessly they watched the light to which they were drawing nearer and nearer. How long would it take the ship to reach it, drifting at this rate?

"Have we got two more hours?" shouted Hudson. Probably not so long, was the reply. Less than two hours.

Hudson went down to his cabin again, tears coming to his eyes as he thought of his father, his mother, his sisters. Never to see them again on this earth. How they would grieve, not knowing what had happened to him when the ship went down. He took out his pocketbook and carefully wrote in his name and address. If his body were found, that would identify him, he thought. Then he looked around for provision having been made, means to save himself from drowning at all. He had not given up all hope of survival. Seeing a hamper which he thought might float, he decided to take it up on deck, and hold on to it tight when the ship went down. He put a few things in it which he thought might be useful if he ever got to land, and struggled up on deck again.

All the time, in his heart, he was praying. He found it almost impossible to frame coherent sentences, for his mind was in a turmoil, but something within went on silently pleading with God, his Father, to save them. He looked at the sea, and saw the waters white with foam in the bright moonlight. Only a few hundred yards ahead of' them, it seemed, was land, and the rocks.

"Can the boats live in a sea like this?" he asked the captain, wondering why they were not lowered.

"No."

"Couldn't we lash some spars together and make a raft of

it?" suggested Hudson.

"No time." The captain moved suddenly, as though he had made up his mind.

"We must try and turn her, or it's all up," he said. They seemed to be making straight for the land that lay just ahead. "We'll have to tack . . . The sea may sweep the deck in turning, and wash everything overboard . . . but we must try!" and he gave the order. The effort to turn the ship outward failed. The force of the wind and the waves was too strong.

Desperately the captain turned the ship the other way. It meant sailing dangerously near the rocks, but with the added impetus of the wind in the sails, it was just possible they might be cleared. All eyes were on those rocks, with the white foam dashing against them and splashing feet high into the air. Could the ship steer clear?

They were only two ships' length away, and if the little vessel could not hold her course, she would be dashed to pieces within a few minutes. Breathlessly Hudson watched, clinging to the rigging as the ship, tossed up and down, beat her way through the waves. They were passing the rocks. They were passing—they'd passed! Now, could they but beat out to sea, away from that dangerous coast, they might yet be saved.

Then it happened. The wind that had been beating so relentlessly on them, veered in their favor. The change of direction was only slight, to be sure—a mere two points, but it was sufficient to carry them away from the coast at last. When the sun rose on Monday morning it shone down, not as Hudson had feared, on a few broken timbers, but on a little ship, sails gallantly hoisted, making for the open sea.

7
SO THIS IS CHINA

After the excitement and danger of those first days, Hudson was very thankful when the ship entered warmer and calmer regions, where his belongings, saturated with salt water, at last got dried. For weeks that ran into months the little *Dumfries* sailed the oceans, first the Atlantic as she traveled down the west coast of Africa, right across the Indian Ocean to within 120 miles of Australia, and through the straits between the islands of Southeast Asia, leading to the Pacific. Among those islands, Hudson learned that being becalmed can be as dangerous as those of being driven by the wind.

For days the sails of the little ship had been hanging limply from the masts, with scarcely a breeze to stir them. On more than one occasion she had progressed only seven miles in twenty-four hours, and in spite of the interest of see-ing palm-fringed islands on the horizon, or watching the tropical fish that darted through the waters, the voyage was growing tedious. It was nearly five months since he had come on board at Liverpool, and Hudson knew every rope and every plank on the deck of the *Dumfries*. How glad would he be to set foot on dry land again.

One Sunday morning, as he was conducting a service on deck, he noticed that his good friend, the captain, looked worried. He paid less attention to the service than was usual, and every now and then walked over to the rails, look-ing out across the smooth waters. There was not the slightest breeze and when, a little later, the crew had dispersed, and Hudson was standing alone with the captain, he learned the reason for his anxiety. The ship was being carried along by a strong current towards some sunken reefs, and without a wind to fill the sails, there was no way of resisting the power of the waters.

"We are so near the reefs already, that I doubt whether we shall get through the afternoon in safety," the captain told him. At sunset a breeze usually sprang up, but by then the ship would be floundering hopelessly on the jagged, hidden rocks. The only possible hope lay in lowering one of the boats, and endeavoring to tow the ship out of danger. All the efforts of the men, rowing furiously, were in vain, however. The current was too strong, and they could not so much as turn the ship's head.

The captain stood beside Hudson in silence, and then said in as matter-of-fact a voice as he could:

"Well, we've done everything that can be done. We can only wait now."

Quite suddenly, Hudson thought of something. If only the breeze that usually blew up at sunset blew up now, they would be saved. And although they had no power at all over winds and breezes—God had. God could make the breeze blow earlier.

"There is one thing left that we haven't done," he said quietly.

"Oh, what is that?" queried the captain.

They had not prayed. That was the one thing left that remained undone. The captain was silent, and Hudson continued. There were four or five of them on board, out of all the crew, who believed in God and believed that He heard prayer. "Let each one of us go to our cabins, and let us all agree to pray that God will send a breeze now. He can send it just as easily now as this evening."

The captain was a little surprised at the suggestion, but after a moment's hesitation he agreed. Very well, he said, they would do that. He would go to his cabin and pray, and Hudson could find the mate, the steward and the Swedish carpenter, and suggest that they do so, too. They, of all the members of the crew, were known to fear God. Let them do the one thing left that could save the ship.

Hudson had been in his cabin praying for only a short while, when he felt so certain that God was going to send a breeze that he got up from his knees, went on deck, and suggested to the first officer that he let down the corners of the mainsail.

"What would be the good of that?" asked the first officer scornfully. Not unreasonably, he felt he knew more about the time to let down sails than the young "landlubber" before him.

"We have been asking God to send a wind," explained Hudson, "and it's coming immediately."

The first officer fairly snorted. "I'd rather see a wind than hear about it," he retorted forcefully. But instinctively he glanced up towards the sails, and Hudson, following his gaze, saw the corner of the topmost sail flutter.

"Look at the royal!" he exclaimed excitedly. "The wind is coming!"

"It's only a puff," said the officer unbelievingly. He shouted an order, nevertheless, and within a minute barefooted seamen were thudding across the deck, and up into the rigging. The sound of the sudden activity brought the captain up from his cabin to see what was happening. The sails billowed in the breeze, while the ship turned slowly and steadily from the reef to cruise away at six or seven knots. Young Hudson Taylor, his eyes gleaming with joy and his heart brimming over with thankfulness, was quietly rejoicing in his God, who answered prayer.

Less than a month later the *Dumfries* eventually anchored at Gutzlaff island to await the coming of the pilot who was to guide them up the estuary of Shanghai itself. The sunny skies and blue waters of warmer regions were left behind now. Instead, as he stood by the rails, Hudson saw nothing but a thick fog and the sullen-looking waters of the mighty Yangtze, the river that carves its way from the mysterious tableland of Tibet through the fertile, populous plains of China to empty itself at last in the turbulent China Sea.

Hudson peered around him, straining his eyes for a glimpse of the land to which he had come. The fog was too thick to allow him a view of the long, low-lying shore yet, but as he leaned over the rails he discerned the dim outlines of other vessels—strange-looking craft with one enormous sail hanging from the mast, and with curved, curiously painted hulls. There was no mistaking them for anything else but the Chinese junks whose pictures he had studied so often in the illustrated book on China in the old home at Barnsley.

Now he was seeing junks with his own eyes, and as he watched one drew near enough for him to see the men on board. Loose-fitting blue home-spun jackets and trousers, skin the color of old parchment, dark, enigmatic eyes, long thin hair plaited in a pigtail—Chinese. For the first time Hudson looked into the faces of members of the great race to which God had sent him, and among whom he hoped to spend his life. He could not understand a word of their language, and their strangely inexpressive faces betrayed nothing of their feelings. How could he set about learning to speak, he wondered. Where would he go to live when he went ashore on this unknown land? How would he even get anything to eat, since he had no idea what to ask for? He paced the deck, muffled in his warmest clothes, turning these and other questions over in his mind until his reverie was interrupted by the sudden activity on deck.

"The pilot! The pilot's coming aboard!" What excitement! For the first time in five and a half months there was someone who could give them news of the outside world. For the first time in five and a half months, here was another Englishman mounting the gangway. It seemed that everybody on board came on deck to see him. What news he had to give them. In the months they had been sailing, cut off entirely from the outside world, troubles had arisen in Europe which were leading up to war. In China itself was war already—civil war, with great rebel forces sweeping up from the south against the imperial armies that poured down from the north.

As for Hudson and his plans, Shanghai was right in the thick of the fighting. Rebels held the city, which was besieged by an imperial army, of about fifty thousand men. Food was already at famine prices, and the rate of exchange was rising. An English pound sterling, which would previously buy five Chinese dollars, would now only purchase three.

Little wonder that the next day it was with very mixed feelings he stepped ashore, and followed his guide through swarms of bawling, shouting Chinese coolies, to the British consulate. He was in China at last! That was thrilling. But as he picked his way across the mud, he could not but be aware of the difficulties that confronted him. No one was expecting him, he had not one friend in the whole of Shanghai, and he had very little money. He had three letters of introduction to people living in Shanghai, however, which he planned to present as soon as possible. Apart from that, he had no idea what he ought to do, but he had arrived at last! The dangers of the sea voyage seemed insignificant compared with the extreme sense of loneliness that now came over him. Once at the consulate, the replies to his inquiries after the men to whom his letters of introduction were

50

addressed only served to make matters worse.

The first man, he learned, had died of fever a month or two previously. The second had already returned to America. Only the third was known still to be in Shanghai—and the letter of introduction to him had been given Hudson by a comparative stranger. With a sinking heart, he set off to the compound of the London Missionary Society.

He walked for over a mile through streets which got narrower and narrower as he left the European quarter behind. Curved roofs, overhanging balconies, tiny, dark little shops with ornate, swinging signs, all seemed so strange to the Yorkshire lad as he made his way past them. He was surrounded by dark-eyed, seemingly mysterious, unsmiling Chinese. Coolies swung along with baskets dangling from both ends of the poles slung across their shoulders, gasping out sing-song warnings as they wound their way through the crowds. Pig-tailed men lounged in the open-fronted shops and restaurants that lined the narrow streets. Vendors of steaming, savory foods stood by their little portable stalls, ready to provide a meal at a moment's notice. Every now and then the crowds pressed back to make room for a sedan chair carried by running coolies, only to swarm into the street again when it had passed.

Hudson was to become so accustomed to such scenes in the years that lay ahead that they became as familiar as the market square at Barnsley, but on this, his first day in China, it all seemed unreal, almost fantastic. With a sense of relief, mingled with some apprehension, he arrived at last at the large double gates of the mission compound.

A Chinese doorkeeper, hands tucked in his sleeves, bowed to the young Westerner. "Master wanted who?"

Hudson produced his letter of introduction and asked to see Dr. Medhurst.

"Doctor not at home. Doctor gone away." The gatekeeper,

respectful but remote, bowed apologetically.

"Where has he gone?" asked Hudson. The gatekeeper apparently had exhausted his stock of English. He just did not understand.

This was a predicament! It was already evening, and before long it would be dark. Alone in a strange city, unable to speak a word of Chinese, what was he to do? He tried again to make the gatekeeper understand, but without success. He was on the verge of giving up when, to his relief, he saw a young man who was obviously European walking across the compound. Hudson lost no time in introducing himself.

"My name is Edkins," said the young man pleasantly. "Dr. Medhurst is not here, but his colleague is, and I am sure he will be glad to help you. Please come in and sit down, while I go and fetch him."

That night, when Hudson eventually went to bed, it was neither in the bunk in his little cabin on the *Dumfries*, nor in some Chinese inn among people whose language he could not understand, but in a comfortable, clean bed in a large, airy room on the London Missionary Society compound.

8

SING FOR YOUR LIFE

The three young missionaries sat down somewhat wearily, though cheerfully, in one of the native junks drawn up by the muddy river bank, and mopped their faces as the boatmen pulled away from the shore. It had been a full day for them. Setting out from Shanghai after breakfast, they had arrived at Woosung Island about noon, and from that time until now had been distributing tracts, and talking as best they could with their limited knowledge of Chinese to the boatmen along the shore. The junks that plied the waterways around Shanghai were innumerable. Large and small, new and old, housing families whose whole lives were spent in their little floating homes, they had attracted the attention of Hudson Taylor and his friends, Edkins and Quarterman.

"We really ought to go and tell them about Christ," they decided. How could these poor people with their little god-shelves and sticks of incense turn from idol worship and superstition if they never heard of the one true God? They had set out on a day's missionary activity among them, glad enough to be free for a few hours from the grind of language study. They were pleased with themselves now, as they relaxed, lulled by the gentle lapping of the water on the sides of the boat.

The junk dwellers they had met had been friendly and willing enough to receive the neat little booklets handed to them, written in their own language. Some had even assured the young missionaries that having read them themselves, they would pass them on to others, at the ports to which they were going. It had been a day well spent, and now, as evening drew on, if they could get past the Chinese imperial fleet safely, they would be back in Shanghai before dark.

But could they get past the imperial fleet safely? The boatmen were decidedly apprehensive about it, and not at all pleased that the three honorable gentlemen had left it so late to return. It was comparatively safe for native junks to cross the waters during the daytime, but to float around after dark, under the very noses of the imperial guns, was different. The imperial guns had a habit of going off with very little provocation, and anything seen moving on the waters after dark was liable to be suspected of belonging to the rebels. It was much too late to be setting out on the return journey, and the boatmen did not like it. Even the missionaries were feeling slightly uneasy.

"If they know we are English and American, it will be all right," said Hudson. Belonging to the neutral Western powers, whose warships were at anchor in the harbor, and whose armed men were ready to protect their life and property should they be attacked, they could move about in comparative safety. "But how are they to know, when it is dark?" White skins and light hair could not be seen after dark. Only their voices could betray that they were not Chinese then. Only their voices... Suddenly Edkins had an idea.

"I know," he said. "We'll sing. We'll all sing together at the tops of our voices in English, and they'll know we are Westerners." A good idea. Their throats were somewhat dry and strained, for they had already sung and talked a lot that day, in the course of their missionary activities, but they did their best, and as they approached some ships that appeared to be the imperial fleet they started going through their repertoire. They sang all the hymns that they could remember, thankful to observe that they were passing ship after ship without being challenged.

They were just lapsing into silence, the last ship having been passed, when the boatmen said urgently, "Again sing! Again sing!"

Why? They were only now approaching the imperial fleet, they were told, the ships they had just passed were harmless cargo boats. "Quick! Quick! Sing! Sing!" hissed the boatmen.

"'The spacious firmament on high," gasped Edkins, and burst into song, the other two accompanying him. Over the waters three young voices floated, proclaiming sturdily that "the blue ethereal sky, the unwearied sun, the moon, and the stars that round her burn, in reason's ear they all rejoice, and utter forth a glorious voice, for ever singing as they shine, the hand that made us is divine!"

It took three verses of eight lines each to advertise it adequately, and the last line was sung over twice, which certainly helped to spin it out. But alas! They reached their triumphant conclusion just as they were passing the largest ship in the fleet. "The hand that made us is divine" was followed by silence, as the three songsters sat breathing somewhat heavily after their exertions. Then, from the imperial vessel was heard the ominous sound of an alarm gong being frantically beaten.

"What next?" cried Edkins. "We must go on singing. There's not a moment to lose." Without waiting for a suggestion, he started singing again. Simultaneously Hudson began singing something else, while Quarterman, evidently inspired by the situation, struck up, "Blow ye the trumpet, blow!" to a rollicking tune. The effect of the musical medley on those who listened was not reassuring. The men on the warship shouted, the panic-stricken boatmen yelled explanations, and for a few moments all were shouting something different at the tops of their voices. The imperial fleet, expecting some rebel treachery, prepared to repel any attack. And the missionaries, realizing that the guns were in all likelihood being trained on them, heard an authoritative voice from the ship demanding, "Who goes there?"

"Great English Nation!" chorused Hudson and Edkins in reply.

"Flowery Flag Country!" boomed Quarterman, the American.

"White devils! White devils!" yelled the boatmen. "White devils on board!"

"Where going?" came from the imperial ship.

"Shanghai."

"Doing what?"

"Preaching their religion. White devils preaching their religion," explained the boatmen. This singular announcement might have been expected to produce panic, but strangely enough, it had the reverse effect. The imperial fleet grasped the situation, and the boat was permitted to proceed.

"What do you mean by calling us white devils?" demanded the missionaries as they drew away from the fleet. "We may be white, but we are not devils," they said severely. "We are men of flesh and blood, created by the one true God, as you are. Devils are without bodies, and cannot be seen. Furthermore, they are evil spirits, enemies of the one true God, full of wicked intent towards mankind. Devils indeed! Surely you can see we are not devils but men like yourselves!"

The boatmen were very apologetic, especially as they had not yet received their money. They had grossly offended the three honorable lords, they said. They had been greatly afraid when the commander of the ship had flown into such a fierce temper, and did not know what they were saying. Also, they were but low and uncultured fellows, and could not read a single letter, never having been to school. The exalted countries from which the honorable lords emanated were places of great learning and wisdom, unlike the poor and despicable land to which they had now come. They, the unworthy boatmen, had been greatly enlightened since the honorable lords had condescended to sit in their poor vessel and speak words of priceless wisdom. Never again, they asserted, under any amount of pressure, would they ever refer to the eminent and exalted ones from the Great British Nation and the Flowery Flag Country in such a way.

The missionaries tried to explain that they were not offended, only anxious that they should be recognized as human beings who had come to them with a message from the one true God. They parted on the shore on the best of terms. That evening, as the boatmen squatted down with bowls and chopsticks to enjoy their evening meal of steamed rice, they agreed that the white devils were really very artless and harmless. If they were somewhat unreasonable, they were generous with their money.

Hudson hurried away as quickly as possible when they landed, for he was afraid he would not be in time to cross the creek to the native city where he was living. Indeed, he arrived just as the last plank of the drawbridge was being withdrawn, and returned to his home tired, hungry and happy. Sitting down in his little whitewashed room he tackled his evening meal with zest. It consisted of a bowl of steamed rice, and four little plates of Chinese vegetables and chopped meat, eaten with chopsticks instead of with knife and fork. Already it seemed quite natural to eat that sort of food in that sort of manner, and Hudson did good justice to it before going to bed.

It was nearly a year since he had set sail from Liverpool on the *Dumfries*. For the first few months after landing in Shanghai he had stayed in the hospitable compound of the London Missionary Society, where he had employed a

Chinese man to teach him the language. Now, however, he had left the comfortable security of the international settlement, with its consulates and guards of well-armed European and American soldiers, and was living alone in a ramshackle native house near the north gate of the Chinese city.

He was constantly within the sound and sight of fighting, and the misery and suffering around him were appalling. Whole houses had been destroyed by gunfire, many poor people were homeless, beggars seemed to swarm the streets with their pathetic cries for "Bread! Bread!" It was not unusual to see captured soldiers being dragged along by their pigtails to be beheaded, or to hear their screams as they were tortured.

The street in which he lived was one which the Imperial troops had threatened to burn, and every night Hudson went to bed realizing that he might have to run for his life before morning came. He always saw that his swimming belt was properly blown up before he went to sleep, for in the event of a sudden attack, he decided he would jump with it into the creek, and swim across to the international settlement.

It was an eerie feeling to be alone in the upper rooms of the old house, with its innumerable passages and outhouses, in such circumstances. Many times he would turn to his Bible to read some comforting passage before kneeling to pray. As he did so, however, he found that his fears were calmed. It was as though the strong, reassuring Voice of a protecting Presence spoke to him, and he went to sleep as peacefully as he had when he was a child with his mother telling him a story until he fell asleep.

In spite of the constant danger, and the poverty and sorrow which surrounded him, he was happier now that he was actually living right among the Chinese people than he had been with other Europeans in the settlement. There was a deep satisfaction in being able to do something to help these sufferers in their distress. His medical knowledge was already coming in useful, and better still, he was now able to talk Chinese a little, which meant he could speak about God, and his Son, Jesus Christ.

He employed a Chinese Christian to run a little day school for children, and with this man Hudson went out into the narrow streets with their overhanging balconies and ornate swinging signs, distributing tracts and talking to such people as were prepared to listen. Yes, he was beginning to do the very work he had come to China to do, and the thought of having to leave it saddened him. Yet he realized that he would probably have to do so.

The fighting was drawing nearer almost daily, and the rebel cannons were now at the end of the very street in which he was living, in preparation for defending it against the Imperial army. Had he had only himself to consider, he might well have decided to remain on and face what was coming. But the Chinese Evangelization Society sent word that they were sending out another worker, for whom Hudson was expected to make preparation — Dr. Parker who was already on his way to Shanghai with his wife and three small children. To bring another man to live with him in this dangerous place was one thing—to bring a mother with helpless little children here was another. Unless the situation improved, Hudson knew he would have to move back to the settlement.

One night, having slept for a few hours, he was awakened with a start by the sound of a crackling and a roaring, and by a strange light reflected in his room. It was a fire! Wooden houses, one joining another in the narrow street, meant a fire spread rapidly. In less time than it takes to tell, Hudson was out of his bed and bundling into his clothes. There was a wind blowing, to make matters worse, and the dull red glow reflected in his room seemed to be growing brighter.

He decided to climb up on the roof to see just where the fire was, and to his horror he saw it was apparently only a few houses away. He also heard the all-too-familiar sound of shooting, and even as he looked around from his vantage point on the tiles, bullets splattered on the buildings around him. He crouched lower, his eyes still fixed on the fire. He could see the spirals of smoke and flames spurting over the curved roofs, and hear the sounds of excited talking and shouting in the street. What was actually happening he could not see, but he prayed silently and urgently that his heavenly Father would protect him.

As he was praying, drops of rain began to fall. Suddenly a cannonball struck the roof of the house opposite, and fragments of the tiles flew past him. It dawned on him that his present position was neither safe nor comfortable! He climbed back into his room once more, thankful that the rain was falling more steadily, and the wind had dropped. The fire gradually subsided. By five o'clock in the morning, the immediate danger was past and Hudson crept back into bed to sleep for an hour or two before starting the work of the day.

Shooting and fighting were almost a nightly occurrence now, so there was nothing to do but to procure a home for the Parkers and their three children in the international settlement. After many fruitless searches in the overcrowded area, he was able to rent three rooms on the first floor of one of the houses in the London Missionary Society compound. Two days later the Parkers arrived, and Hudson, aged twenty-two, after barely eight months experience in China, found himself responsible for a family.

9

THE MAN IN THE WALL

The Parkers were strong, sensible Scots, prepared to put up with inconveniences—and inconveniences met them at every turn. Three upstairs rooms might have proved adequate accommodation for them had the three rooms been suitably furnished with beds, cupboards and chests of drawers. Unfortunately, they were not.

All Hudson seemed to possess in the way of furniture was a Chinese bed, two tables and half a dozen chairs. These, of course, were placed unreservedly at the disposal of the family, but Mrs. Parker looked round in vain for somewhere to put clothes, shoes, bottles and books. There wasn't one shelf in the house. Furthermore, there were no carpets on the floor, the windows were bare, and although it was winter, there was no fire.

It was, to say the least of it, rather a cheerless place after a long and uncomfortable sea voyage, for the family with three small children to come to. Poor Hudson, when he saw what the rooms looked like piled up with boxes, baskets and bundles, was overwhelmed with shame and confusion. He had not realized it would be as bad as that. Even if he had, it would have made little difference. The fact was that after paying the first installment of rent, he had less than three dollars left. He devoutly hoped that Dr. Parker would be adequately supplied with funds, for otherwise he was not at all sure where next week's food would come from. It was distinctly disconcerting, therefore, to learn that his new colleague only had a few dollars, and was expecting to find money awaiting him in Shanghai. The Chinese Evangelization Society had assured him they would send him some there.

No money was awaiting him, however. Letters there contained greetings and advice, but no mention of funds. As Hudson had already discovered, the financial arrangements of the Chinese Evangelization Society were extremely haphazard. There seemed to be an unexpressed conviction on the part of its leaders that when missionaries had run out of money, they could happily and healthily live on air until more money was sent to them.

Fortunately, this view was not shared by the firm of agents who transmitted the Society's funds. When they realized the predicament Hudson and his newly-arrived colleagues were in, they lent them money until they should receive funds from the proper quarter. Hudson was thankful for this timely help—nor did he entirely disagree with the few tart comments the agents made about the business arrangements of the Chinese Evangelization Society.

He wrote the Society a frank though respectful letter, containing a few stiff phrases about their responsibilities to their missionaries, and then settled down as best he could, to accommodate himself to his new conditions. For the next few months he lived with the Parkers. He was glad for such earnest and self-sacrificing fellow workers as they proved to be. Living with a family of five in three rooms was not conducive to quiet concentration on studying one of the world's most difficult languages, however. Many times he longed for the ramshackle house near the North Gate of the Chinese city, where he had constant contact with the Chinese themselves. That was the way to get to know them, to learn to speak as they spoke; to live among them. He was absolutely delighted when his friend Edkins made a suggestion to him one day.

"I'm going to take a trip down to Ka-shing," he said to Hudson. "I shall hire a native houseboat for about a week and travel slowly, stopping at the towns and cities we pass to give out tracts and do some preaching. Will you come along with me?"

Would he! Hudson required no persuasion. To travel inland for a week, to live on a Chinese boat, to see Chinese life at first hand—this was the very thing he had come for. Without delay he made his preparations, and quite considerable they needed to be—bedclothes, baskets of food, fuel, a cooking stove, saucepans, as well as his medicines and a large assortment of books and tracts. As he walked down to the crowded shore behind the coolies he had hired to carry his baggage to the boat, he marveled that so many things were required for so short a time.

After bargaining and shouting and scrambling, everything was safely on board and the boat drew away, winding its way between the innumerable junks anchored by the shores and into midstream. By this time, Hudson was getting used to the customs of coolies, and was not unduly perturbed when they yelled at each other, hurling epithets which he mercifully did not understand. They usually parted as affably as if they had merely been making inquiries about each other's health, he observed, and as if it was all in the day's work.

Now sailing along the broad waterways, Hudson gazed at the low-lying shore with its muddy banks and squalid-looking shacks, until gradually the scene changed as they drew away from the city towards the open country. Village after village they passed, and great tracts of land where innumerable mounds in the ground marked the graves of generations past. How thickly populated this country was, thought Hudson, as he looked at those shores.

Little groups of houses clustered together every mile or

two, and everywhere could be seen the signs of human habitation. When they eventually arrived at the first city where they were to go ashore, they were immediately surrounded by swarms of the blue-clad sons of Han, staring with undisguised interest at the two foreigners. Grasping as many tracts and booklets as they could conveniently hold, Hudson and Edkins made their way up the bank and into the city.

While they were there, in that first city on their trip, they saw something which lived long in Hudson's memory. They had entered the courtyard of a temple, with its dragon ornamented roof and its gloomy halls where enormous, fearsome-looking idols looked down impassively on the worshippers who bowed before them. The crowd that gathered around them listened quietly enough as Edkins and Hudson preached in turn. When they had finished speaking, they had no difficulty in disposing of the booklets they had with them. They were just about to move on when two or three of the priests, clad in rather dingy yellow robes and with clean-shaven heads, approached them.

"Honorable gentlemen, please come inside and sit down for a while," they invited politely, leading the way into their own living quarters. The two missionaries, interested to see the inside of a Buddhist monastery, accompanied them willingly. After a short conversation, the priests offered to show them around, and then said, "Would you like to come and see our holy man?"

Holy man? Who and what was he, the missionaries wondered? Yes, they said. They would indeed like to see the "holy man." They were led to a remote part of the monastery and up to a wall. In the wall was a small opening, just large enough for a man's hand to pass through.

"He is in there," said the priests. Hudson looked for a door, but saw none. "There is no door," he was told. Almost incredulously Hudson realized that whoever was in there was bricked in! Peering through the opening he could dimly make out the figure of a man, huddled against the wall. There was no window, so the only light that entered was that which made its way in from the gloomy hall. There he was, a human being like himself, alone in that tiny room which was indeed his coffin.

He still breathed, and ate and drank the food passed to him through the hole in the wall, but apart from that, he might have been dead. In the dimness and the silence he passed his days and nights alone. By so doing, by cutting himself off from the fellowship of his fellow creatures, would he not crush his sins, would he not achieve holiness and accumulate much merit, as every natural desire was stifled? Certainly his religion taught him so, and he was already an object of great veneration in the city. Quite voluntarily he had entered upon the living death, believing that thereby he would attain nirvana, the "heaven" of the Buddhists.

Edkins and Hudson exchanged significant glances. They had heard of these holy men, poor devotees of their religion, but had never before seen one. Moved by a feeling of deep compassion, Edkins went near to the hole, to be better able to speak to the man inside. He had come to him with a message from the one true God, he explained, and very earnestly he told the "holy man" that his sins could be freely forgiven, for Christ's sake. As clearly as he could, Edkins spoke of Jesus on the cross, and of his rising again from the dead, to be the Savior of those who trusted in Him. It was all strange and new to the man behind the wall, and to the yellow-clad priests standing around. Never had they heard this "foreign religion" before, and they gazed at the two missionaries with dark, impassive eyes, and politely disbelieving faces.

They had their god—Buddha. The Westerners evidently had their god—Jesus. Good, good. It was all good. It mattered not what religion it was, all led to the way, they said. They accompanied their two visitors to the gate of the temple courtyard, bowed affably, and returned to the dark building with its fitfully flickering oil lamps, its incense sticks and fearsome idols, and its "holy man" in his dark stillness.

Hudson and Edkins emerged into the street, and almost immediately became the center of attraction again. They had to return to their boat two or three times to load up again with tracts, and on one occasion narrowly escaped being trapped on the water's edge by the crowds that swarmed around them. It was not until evening was drawing on that they had an opportunity to be quiet, and review the happenings of the day. Climbing up the winding stairs inside a pagoda, they stood together looking down silently on the scene below.

The city looked like a lake of roof-tops from their high vantage point, and they could see across them to the stout, solid walls encircling the city and the flat countryside beyond. The paddy-fields, profusely sprinkled with clumps of trees that indicated the presence of villages, stretched right away to the horizon. Here and there pagodas and temples with curved roofs standing out against the sky told of other cities and towns not far away.

Hundreds of thousands of human beings were living within the range of their vision, they realized, as they stood watching the evening shadows lengthen over the innumerable dark little homes with their idols and their paper gods, their incense sticks and their ancestral tablets. This was only on the very fringe of the great unreached empire that stretched away for hundreds of miles into the unexplored interior.

The interior—inland China.

As Hudson stood in the pagoda that evening, the immensity of China's population began to have a new meaning for him. Shanghai with its narrow native streets and teeming markets had more or less been the limits of his vision until now, although he and Dr. Parker had many times walked miles out into the country to preach and distribute tracts in the villages around.

Now, however, looking over the great silent plain, he became dimly aware of regions away towards the west, great tracts of land where cities, towns, markets and villages lay in a profusion that defied the imagination. In them all, the only way the people knew was the dark way of death. He remembered that silent, walled-up man in the monastery. The temple gongs, the worship of ancestor spirits, the fear of demons—like a pall they seemed to hang over this great eastern civilization. It seemed to be lying hopelessly in the arms of some immense, evil monster.

The boy who had heard a voice saying "Go for me to China" began to comprehend as never before the greatness of the task before him. At the same time, his very soul steeled itself for the battle. Here was a conflict that was going to demand every ounce of his strength, that required courage and determination above anything he had imagined. It was in a solemn frame of mind that he returned to the boat that evening. Whatever it cost, however rough the way, the people of this land must be told of the only One who could save them from death.

10
THIEVES

Hudson sat down wearily on the temple steps, and decided he would have to spend the rest of the night there. It was already past one o'clock in the morning, and he had searched in vain for a place to sleep in the unfriendly city. All doors seemed closed against him, and he was too exhausted to walk any more. He stretched himself out on the cold, uneven stones, put his little bag of money under his head, and wondered if he would be able to sleep.

With his long blue gown, cloth slippers and, above all, a clean-shaven head from the crown of which dangled a long pigtail, he looked as much like a Chinese man as a fair-skinned, blue-eyed Yorkshire youth could look. Months ago he had taken the step of dressing exactly as the Chinese did. He had called down a good deal of criticism on himself from fellow Europeans for it, but he was able to mingle much more freely with the Chinese themselves, and had traveled extensively in places where most Europeans would have been mobbed.

This was the first time he had ever had to sleep out of doors. Somehow, things seemed to have been going all wrong lately. First there was the fire which had destroyed all his medicines—a serious loss, for they would be very expensive to replace. Then there was the disappearance of his servant and all his luggage two days ago, leaving him stranded with nothing but the clothes he was wearing. Now, there was the crowning misfortune of being unable to find a lodging. Well, when day broke he would have some breakfast, make a final search for the missing servant and luggage, and then return to Shanghai. It would be futile to attempt to reach Ningpo, where the Parkers were now living, with the small amount of money left. He pressed his face into his hard, knobby pillow, sighed sleepily and closed his eyes.

Suddenly he was wide awake, his body tense but motionless. What was that moving in the darkness? A dim figure was coming stealthily across the wide steps towards him, and Hudson, still lying as though asleep, could see the ragged form of a beggar. The man crept silently to the form of the recumbent missionary, and stood looking down at him. Hudson did not move, and after a minute or two, evidently assured that he was asleep, the beggar bent down and began gently feeling him.

"What do you want?"

Hudson spoke quietly, but there was an ominous ring in his voice. The beggar was taken by surprise. The man lying there wasn't asleep after all—indeed, he sounded very much awake, as though he were prepared to take immediate action. The beggar beat a hasty retreat.

Hudson decided his money should be in a safer place than under his sleeping head, so having put some of it in an inner pocket, and the rest up his sleeve, settled down again. He was just dozing off when some instinct once more aroused him. He was conscious of movements in the darkness, the dim outlines of silent figures approaching. The beggar had returned with a companion or two. Again Hudson lay motionless until he felt a hand moving behind his head, feeling for the bag of cash.

"What do you want?" he asked in the same quiet but significant tones as before. He received no answer, but the beggars retreated a couple of steps, and sat down.

"What are you doing?" demanded Hudson.

"Spending the night here outside the temple—like you," came the reply.

"Then kindly go over to the other side, and leave me alone," said Hudson. "There is plenty of room for you there."

The men made no reply to this suggestion, but did not move. Hudson therefore sat up. It was useless lying there, where he might drop off to sleep. He would certainly be robbed of all he had left unless he kept his wits about him.

"You'd better lie down and sleep," said one of the beggars, disarmingly, "or else you'll not be able to work tomorrow. Don't be afraid," he continued reassuringly. "We won't leave you. We'll see no one does you any harm."

"You listen to me," said Hudson stoutly. "I don't want your protection. I don't need it. I am not a Chinese, and I don't worship lifeless idols. I worship God, he is my Father and I trust in him. He will protect me. I know what you are, and what you intend doing. I tell you, I shall not go to sleep. I intend keeping my eye on you.

The beggars did not move, and neither did Hudson. Sitting with his back to the wall, trying not to nod off to sleep, the hours passed slowly. Every now and then he made a remark, partly to make the men realize he was still awake, and partly to keep himself that way. Eventually he hit on the idea of keeping himself awake by singing, and when he got tired of that, repeated passages of Scripture aloud, and then prayed. All this did much to cheer him, while having exactly the reverse effect upon the beggars, who grumbled to each other, urged him to be quiet, and finally departed. Just before dawn, seeing they had disappeared down the narrow street, Hudson relaxed and even slept for a little while before the city began to stir.

"Foxes have holes, and the birds of the air have nests; but the Son of man hath nowhere to lay his head." The words had a new meaning for him that day, as he trudged along the track between endless rice-fields on his way to the place where he hoped to get on a boat going to Shanghai. His Master knew what it was to be despised and rejected, as he had been the previous day when searching in vain for a lodging. His Master knew what it was to suffer the cold and discomfort of sleeping out of doors, and to be dogged by unscrupulous men.

How insignificant seemed his own sufferings and humiliations compared with all that Jesus Christ, the Lord of glory, had endured for him. How little it mattered if he had lost all his belongings, as certainly appeared to be the case. The souls of these Chinese people were of infinitely more value than his cherished earthly possessions. Why had he worried so much about them, and cared so little about the souls of these poor, ignorant, sinning people? "Oh, Lord," he prayed as he walked along, "forgive me for all my shortcomings. Help me to do only thy will, help me to follow in thy footsteps." Nothing else mattered much, but to follow in those footsteps, and to become more like his Master.

That night he was invited by friendly boat-people to sleep on board with them, and he was very glad to do so. It was cold without his bedding, but it was a relief to lie down without fear of being robbed. He got up the next morning with a sore throat but a light heart, for all anxiety about his losses was gone. After all, God was well able to restore them to him if that would be for the best, and if not, then he did not want them.

All that remained was to find a boat going to Shanghai, and return there as soon as possible. He would search for his servant and his luggage no more. He set out on the long walk to the town where he hoped to find a boat, and after paying for the breakfast he had in a little wayside inn, he found he had only 810 in "cash" left. It would be just enough to pay his fare and provide him with food for the three or four days it would take to reach Shanghai. Now to find a boat to take him there as soon as possible.

But there was no boat going to Shanghai. There was not even one going as far as Ka-shing Fu, he was told. Hudson tramped from boat office to river bank, asking of any likely individual whether he knew of a boat going in the direction of Shanghai—all in vain. The boats were grounded in the dry river bed, and until rains came and the waters rose, there they must remain. It might be weeks before they could move and he had only enough money to last about five days. He had almost given up hope when suddenly he saw a mail boat, smaller than the heavy cargo junks that lined the river bank, making its way along the narrow stream that still flowed in the middle of the bed. It was going in the direction of Ka-shing Fu.

"Hi!" Hudson started running, weariness and sore feet forgotten. The boat was ahead of him, and he tore along for a mile before he was in earshot.

"Are you going to Ka-shing Fu?" he yelled.

"No," was the reply.

"Are you going in that direction?"

"No."

"Will you take me as far as you are going?" asked Hudson in desperation.

Hudson stopped dead, watching the boat go on. This was the last straw. He felt sick, and a wave of coldness seemed to sweep over him.

"Better sit down," he thought, and sank down on the grassy riverbank, suddenly faint. Then everything went blank.

How long he lay like that he did not know. Gradually he returned to consciousness, and as he did so he heard the sound of voices. They came from the other side of the canal, and as he came to himself he realized they were talking about him.

"He speaks pure Shanghai dialect," someone said—in pure Shanghai dialect. They evidently took him for a native of their own city. The next thing he knew a small boat was coming across the water to fetch him, and he was invited to come on board.

The kindly boat-people heard his story sympathetically. His servant had disappeared with his luggage, he himself had been searching for two days, and now he had only sufficient money to take him back to Shanghai—and there was no boat. They looked pitifully at the weary Westerner who was dressed as they were, and spoke their language like a native. After he had drunk some tea, they gave him warm water to wash his feet. It was with little exclamations of surprise that they saw how blistered they were. His troubles were finally at an end. The captain of the junk gave him food, then found a boat going to Shanghai and offered to pay the fare himself, if necessary. The tide of misfortune had turned at last.

On his arrival back in Shanghai, Hudson set out inquiries about the servant who had disappeared with his luggage—£40-worth of it. Had the man met with difficulties himself—been arrested, perhaps by some unsympathetic official who did not approve of Chinese who worked for Westerners? Or had he just made off with the stuff himself?

It was not long before it became apparent that the latter was the case, and Hudson was strongly advised to have the law on him. Such a man ought to be punished, he was told, and Hudson agreed in theory. However, there was another point to be considered. He had many times preached to his servants of the love of God, of the forgiveness which the Lord Jesus Christ showed even to those who nailed him to the cross. Here was his opportunity to demonstrate that spirit of forgiveness himself, by returning good for evil. Instead of putting the case into the hands of a Chinese mandarin, therefore, he wrote his servant a letter pointing out the wrong he had done and urging him to change his ways.

How much more important it was, thought Hudson, that the man's conscience should be touched, that he should turn to God and his soul be saved from hell, than that he should get back £40-worth of baggage. If only this act of forgiveness would have that effect on the man, how willingly would Hudson be deprived of twice the amount he had lost—if he had twice the amount which he lost. In point of fact, he hadn't. Having posted the letter, he set about selling what sticks of furniture he still had left in order to make up as best he could the indispensable possessions he had lost, before setting out once more for Ningpo.

Just as he was preparing to leave, news came that a mail-boat had arrived from England. The arrival of a mail-boat was always hailed with joy by the European community, and Hudson was as eager as anyone else to collect the letters that he hoped would be awaiting him at the agent's office. He had to endure a few supercilious glances from top-hatted gentlemen who had also arrived to collect their mail, and who viewed the pig-tailed Englishman in Chinese clothes with undisguised scorn. He was getting accustomed to that. He received his letters, and returning home eagerly scanned them. Would there be one from his mother, or Amelia, with news of home and Barnsley? Would there, by some good chance, be one from the Chinese Evangelization Society containing his salary? Or one from his friend Ben, perhaps, to say he wanted to come and join him in the work?

Ah! Here was one in a handwriting that was becoming familiar. It was from Mr. Berger, a man who had grown very interested in the work of the young missionary, and whose friendly letters always brought warm encouragement and cheered Hudson's heart. He opened it, and read until he came to the words:

"Please accept the enclosed as a token of love from myself and my dear wife." The enclosed—what was it? Hudson opened out the little slip of pink paper tucked inside the letter and saw with amazement that it was a check made out to him for £40. Hudson just stared at it.

There it was again. Another tangible evidence that God knew all about his affairs. He had lost £40-worth of baggage, and here was the money to replace it—sent out from England at least six weeks before he had even been robbed. (He little knew then that another such sum was soon to be on its way from someone else, too.) How glad he was that he had taken no steps to have his servant punished for stealing his things. As he set out again through the beautiful province of Chekiang, with its orchards and steep little hills, its willows and its paddy-fields, he felt like a boy who had passed another examination, and heard the ring of commendation in his Master's voice as he said, "Well done!"

11

MARIA

Miss Aldersey was a wonderful woman. Everyone in Ningpo agreed about that, Chinese and Westerners alike. Indeed, the Chinese regarded her as being of far greater importance than the British consul who, they asserted, invariably obeyed her commands. Rumors hinted that she was endued with magical powers. Were not the earthquake tremors which recently occurred due to the fact that she had opened a mysterious bottle containing a potent charm at five o'clock one morning on the city wall? Weren't other strange phenomena also due to the Honorable Teacher Aldersey's occult power? No doubt the Queen of England, a remarkable woman herself, had appointed Miss Aldersey to rule those of her subjects who had gravitated to the Chinese port city of Ningpo. Of course the British consul obeyed her! Yes, said the Chinese, Miss Aldersey was a wonderful woman.

The European community thought so, too. While they did not attribute the earthquake to her, knowing full well that her bottle contained nothing more devastating than smelling salts, they felt that she did something more noteworthy than that every day of her life. At five o'clock in the morning, winter or summer, rain or shine, she went for a walk on the city wall. It mattered not to her if it were pitch dark. She merely instructed a servant to accompany her with a lantern, and went out as usual for her daily exercise. At five o'clock in the morning. It would have required more than a mere earthquake tremor to persuade the European community to do likewise. Yes, if for that feat alone, they agreed she was a wonderful woman. But that was not all.

This pioneer woman missionary in Ningpo, founder of the first Protestant school for girls in China, had a capacity for work which left frailer mortals breathless. She would listen to her pupils reading their lessons to her even while she was eating her meals. As for holidays, she would take none of them. Other missionaries might go off to the seaside to regain health and strength after their exertions, but Miss Aldersey got the sea breezes by climbing to the ninth story of a tall pagoda, and sniffing them from there. By taking some of her pupils with her, she was able to continue their lessons without interruption. A remarkable woman, without doubt, and if the British consul did not always do exactly what she wanted, he certainly would not have dared to let her know.

It was most unfortunate for Hudson, therefore, that such an influential and awe-inspiring person as the admirable Miss Aldersey should have taken a deep, strong and unshakable dislike to him. Such, however, was the case. The very mention of his name was sufficient to stiffen her little body with what she considered wholly righteous indignation. For Hudson Taylor had actually had the nerve, the audacity, the unimaginable brashness, to propose to Maria.

Maria was the orphan daughter of a missionary, and she was one of the teachers in Miss Aldersey's school. A very useful teacher she was, too, fond of children, and speaking Chinese like a native. She was rather pretty, and Hudson was not the first young man who felt that the name Maria would look better in front of his surname than in front of her own. However, Miss Aldersey did not hold that against her, for the girl could not help it. To give Miss Aldersey her due, she was quite prepared to part with her attractive, efficient young teacher if a really suitable man appeared on the scene. But

Hudson Taylor? The man with the Chinese clothes and a pigtail? A pigtail of his own hair, mind you, dangling from the crown of his head. Who was he, anyhow? A poor, young, unconnected nobody. A fanatic, completely undependable, whom no reputable missionary society would ever employ. Marry Maria? Never! He clearly wanted her money.

Poor nineteen-year-old Maria was overwhelmed. As far as her own feelings were concerned, the idea of marrying Hudson, pigtail or no pigtail, appealed to her strongly. Truth to tell, it had occurred to her several weeks before Hudson had even mentioned it, although, needless to say, she had kept it to herself. Now, however, in the face of Miss Aldersey's anger and powerful reasons, she felt helpless. At that lady's dictation, Maria sat down and wrote a curt letter to say that the proposal was wholly impossible, adding that if Hudson had any gentlemanly feeling at all, he would never again refer to the subject. Miss Aldersey took the letter off in triumph, Maria went to her room and burst into tears, and Hudson, who had expected a more favorable reply, felt as though a door had been slammed, loudly and finally, in his face.

It was not easy to settle down to live and work in Ningpo after that rebuff, but Hudson knew that he must do so. He had already obtained possession of a shop which made an excellent preaching-hall, and was living, not with the Parkers who were in charge of a hospital, but with a young couple, Mr. and Mrs. Jones, who had recently arrived in China. Hudson's days were full, preaching, visiting Chinese who were inquiring about this "Jesus religion" and doing medical work. He was glad his days were busy. He was very lonely. His hopes of companionship all seemed to crash, one by one. When first he came to China he had hoped that before very long his sister Amelia would come and join him. He was fond of Amelia, for all his teasing, and felt she would have been just the one to run the home for him, and work among the Chinese women. Then he had been encouraged by letters from his friend Ben, who was evidently deeply interested in his experiences. Perhaps he would come. It was somewhat of a shock, therefore, when he received the news that Amelia and Ben had got engaged, and were settling down at home, so neither would be coming. Now that Maria who, it must be admitted, he had felt would make an even better companion than either of them, had turned him down, he was bereft beyond words.

The days of early summer, were sad for him. He was perplexed. He had prayed a great deal about the matter before he had gone so far as to propose to Maria. It was strange that things should have taken the turn they had, when he had felt convinced he was doing the right thing. Somehow, try as he would, the feeling that it was the right thing still persisted. He would have been quite certain about it, had he been able to hear poor little Maria's daily prayers, as she knelt by her bedside, morning and night. She very much wanted to be Mrs. Hudson Taylor.

Hudson, however, knew nothing about that. All he had to go on was Maria's letter, and that had been so final, so hopeless. Certainly, he knew he was intended to regard it as such, but the more he thought about it, the more he felt he couldn't. It was her writing, but it was not her way of putting things. He began to wonder if it was not more like Miss Aldersey's way of putting things. If only, thought Hudson, it were possible to see Maria when Miss Aldersey was not around. But in old China custom forbade an unmarried man to try to meet an unmarried woman, so his hands were tied. Their paths rarely crossed. The one effort he had made to talk to her misfired, and he found himself left with someone else, while Maria was whisked away in a sedan-chair.

Eventually he decided there was nothing he could do

about it. His pigtail dangled disconsolately through the hot, sticky June days, as he went about the narrow streets, and preached for an hour or so each evening in the "Jesus Hall." He could not but realize that were he to cut off his braid, he would be regarded as being a much more suitable match for Maria. Cutting it off, however, would mean he could no longer move freely among the Chinese, who regarded him almost as one of themselves.

He knew why he had heard that voice "Go for me to China." There was a work for him to do in this land, and that work was to spread abroad the knowledge of the only One who can save from eternal death. There were towns and cities, villages and hamlets lying in the interior, that were waiting for that news, and he must go. The pigtail must remain. But as Hudson knelt by his bedside, night and morning, praying for the Chinese, the name of "Maria" was also mentioned with earnestness, before he rose from his knees.

Then, quite suddenly in the middle of July, the whole situation was changed by an unexpected rain. It was amazingly well-timed. The storm came sweeping up the river one afternoon when Mrs. Jones was entertaining all the lady missionaries in Ningpo in her home. It broke over Ningpo in a startling deluge, followed by torrential rain. In no time all the streets were running with water and emptied of people. Water poured off roofs and formed ponds and pools in unexpected places, and the ladies looked out of the windows of Mrs. Jones' drawing-room and wondered how and when they would get home again.

It was much later than usual that some sedan-chair carriers eventually arrived at the front gates, their trousers rolled up over their knees, and water dropping from the wide brims of their coolie hats. Even then, there were more ladies than chairs. So, some ladies had to stay behind, while some were carried home. Among those who were carried home was Miss Aldersey. Among those who still awaited sedan-chairs was Maria. There she was when Hudson and Mr. Jones arrived home from the preaching hall.

A smallish drawing-room in which three or four people are sitting is not considered an ideal place for a proposal of marriage, especially from someone who has already been rejected. Hudson realized that, so his intention in making use of this rare opportunity of seeing Maria without Miss Aldersey was merely to ask politely if he might write to her guardian in London for permission to cultivate her acquaintance.

However, once he started, he found himself saying more than that, in spite of onlookers. Maria, usually rather quiet and reserved, responded with surprising and encouraging warmth. In a remarkably short time the position was made quite clear. When the sedan-chairs arrived to convey the remaining ladies through the muddy streets to their homes, no one in the drawing-room misunderstood. Young Hudson Taylor had Maria's full permission and approval to write to her guardian. Although no such thought was put into words, it was clear to all that not even the strongest of Miss Aldersey's earthquakes would prevent him from writing that letter.

Hudson wasted no time in writing to Maria's guardian, but it was over four months before he received a reply. His wasn't the only letter that the mail-boat carried from Ningpo to London addressed to Mr. Tarn. Miss Aldersey wrote to him, too. Mr. Tarn did some discreet research on Hudson before committing himself. Once he finished, he decided that if his niece and ward wanted to marry this young missionary with a pigtail, there was no reason why she should not do so. He only stipulated that as she was now already over twenty, she should wait until she came of age before taking the step. Less than a year after that rainy afternoon, Hudson and Maria were married and settled into the attic over the preaching chapel in Bridge Street.

Bridge Street, Ningpo, was as suitably named as Drainside, Hull, had been, for it was a narrow thoroughfare which started with a bridge and ended with a bridge. As one of them spanned a canal, which ran along at the back of his home, Hudson had plenty to remind him of the old days. He had first moved into this attic when he was a lonely bachelor, and one morning had awakened to find everything covered with a thin film of snow, which had drifted in through the tiled roof during the night. He had waited long enough to trace his initials on the coverlet before he stepped gingerly out of bed and got dressed. However, he decided that the place probably needed fixing up a bit before he could bring Maria there. When she arrived, as Mrs. Hudson Taylor, it was partitioned off into four or five little rooms, all of which had ceilings. There, living right among the Chinese, dressing as they did and speaking their language, they settled down to their work.

12

THREE WANGS

Mr. Nee, looking tall and dignified in his well-cut silk gown and wide-sleeved jacket, walked slowly along the narrow street. The coolies with their rough straw hats moved to one side as they saw him approaching. He was obviously a man of learning, one who read and understood the classics. As such, he was entitled to the respect of the ignorant and unlearned.

Those who recognized him knew also that he was a well-to-do businessman, and for this reason, too, the poorer people stood aside. Mr. Nee moved easily along the street with its flagged pathway and its wide, double-leafed doorways, turning over in his mind the uncertainties of life, or more accurately, the uncertainties of death.

What, he wondered, happened after death? The mystery of what lay beyond the grave disturbed him, making him fearful and uneasy. Where was the Way, the Truth that would bring understanding and relief to his perplexed mind?

The clanging of a bell attracted his attention, and he turned to see where the sound came from. One of the double-leafed doorways stood wide open, and as Mr. Nee looked into the courtyard, he saw several people walking across it, and in at the door of a long room. It looked as though some sort of meeting was about to begin.

"What are they doing in there?" he asked a street vendor, standing by his little portable stall.

"That's the Jesus Hall," came the reply. "Foreigners live in there. When they ring that bell, then they worship."

"What do they do when they worship?" asked Mr. Nee.

"They sing, and read from their sacred classics, and then explain what they've been reading."

Mr. Nee looked again at the open doorway, and decided to go in. He would investigate this foreign religion. Perhaps it would explain some of the dark mysteries of life and death. He entered the room, sat down on one of the benches, and looked towards the little raised platform where a young man was standing, reading aloud from a book he was holding in his hands.

At first sight, the young man appeared to be a Chinese, for he was dressed as such, and only his light eyes and white skin betrayed him. Mr. Nee was not so much interested in the young man as in what he was reading, and he listened intently to the story of a conversation a teacher called Jesus had with a man who came to see him at night.

"As Moses lifted up the serpent in the wilderness, even so must the Son of man be lifted up: that whosoever believeth in him should not perish, but have eternal life. For God so loved the world, that he gave his only begotten Son, that whosoever believeth in him should not perish, but have everlasting life. For God sent not his Son into the world to condemn the world; but that the world through him might be saved."

Everlasting life. That was what Mr. Nee wanted. Not to be condemned, but to be saved. He sat in the preaching hall that evening, gripped by what he heard. This Jesus, whom the foreigners worshiped, was God's own Son. He had come from heaven into the world as a man, and died upon a cross, bearing the sins of all the world, and after he had been dead three days, he came to life again. He came out of the tomb. He walked and talked with his friends, and then one day he left the earth and went back to heaven. He would give everlasting life to all who believed in him.

Sitting in that little preaching hall, with its rice-paper windows and rows of wooden benches, Mr. Nee knew without any doubt that this was the Way. Something within him responded unquestioningly to what he heard. His sadness and perplexity departed. When Hudson closed his Bible and stopped preaching, Mr. Nee rose to his feet. All eyes were turned to him as he said, with quiet, oriental gravity:

"I have long sought the truth, as my father did before me, without finding it. I traveled far and near, searching for the Way, but never found it. In the teachings of Confucius, the doctrines of Buddhism and Taoism, I have found no rest. But I have found rest in what we have heard tonight. From now on I am a believer in Jesus."

He was as good as his word. He explained quite simply to his friends why he would worship and burn incense to the gods no more. He obtained a Bible and started studying it, attended the meetings in the little preaching hall, and accompanied the missionaries practically every day when they went out preaching and visiting. He was not the first Chinese who had turned from idols to the living God after hearing Hudson preach, but none, perhaps, had turned so clearly and definitely on the first hearing of the message.

"How long have you had this good news in your honorable England?" he asked Hudson one day.

Hudson hesitated. This Chinese gentleman, who had responded so gladly and readily to the loving invitation of the living God was so eager that others should hear it too.

"Several hundred years," said Hudson, rather reluctant to have to admit it was so long.

"Several hundred years!" exclaimed Nee in amazement. "Is it possible that in your honorable country you have known about Jesus so long, and only now have come to tell us?" In his mind's eye he saw a man he had loved, earnestly reading the classics, eagerly going to the temples to prostrate himself before the still, unresponsive idols, sitting in silent thought and meditation, seeking to understand the mysteries of life and death, a sadly wistful expression on his face.

"My father sought the truth for more than twenty years," he said slowly. "And he died without finding it. Oh, why did you people not come sooner?"

*   *   *   *   *

Through Mr. Nee's enthusiasm in speaking to all he met about Jesus the Lord, Wang the basket-maker also became a believer. Wang was cheerful and impetuous, so his walk with Christ included a few tumbles. Still his sincerity was obvious. He had been accustomed to working seven days a week, of course, like everybody else around him, until he joined the Christians. When he heard, however, that the Living God had ordained that one day out of seven should be set apart as a day of holy rest, he obeyed the command without question. It meant his employer did not give him any food, nor the princely salary of two pence which was paid him for each day's work. Yet Wang was expected to accomplish as much work in his six days as he had previously done in seven. The basket-maker felt himself well repaid for his sacrifice as he sat in the Jesus Hall on Sundays and listened to the amazing stories from the Holy Book. During the busy season, his irate employer informed him that if he wouldn't work for him on Sundays he could not work for him at all. Wang decided that he must look for employment elsewhere.

On Monday morning, therefore, he visited another basket-maker, to try and find another job. No, he was not wanted. He went to another, with the same result. He tramped around the city in vain. Although they were all so busy, none

86

of the basket-makers would employ him. Wang came to the conclusion that the devil was making things hard for him because he was determined to worship, instead of work, on Sundays.

"I must resist him," thought Wang. He was not prepared to take that sort of opposition lying down, for Wang was a strong man. "I will resist him. If he won't let me get other employment, then I'll give my time to plucking souls from his kingdom." He made no more efforts to get a job, but took a bundle of tracts in his hands, and went out into the street to talk to any men he could find who were willing to listen to him preaching about Jesus. That was how he met Wang the farmer.

Wang the farmer, had previously had a remarkable experience. He had been lying alone in his home in the little village of O-Zi, seriously ill, when he heard a voice calling his name. Knowing none of his family were in the house, he clambered slowly off his big, four-poster bed, to go to the door. No one was there. He lay down again, when for the second time he heard his name called. Once more he dragged himself to the door, only to find no one there. Thoroughly frightened, he cowered under the wadded coverlet on his bed. Surely, he thought, this was the voice of the King of Hell, come to warn him that death was approaching.

Then he heard the voice again, and it told him not to be frightened, for he was not going to die. He was going to get well. When he was well, he was to go to the city of Ningpo, thirty miles away, where he would hear of a new religion. This religion, the voice said, would bring him peace of heart.

To everyone's surprise, Wang the farmer did get well. Remembering his instructions, he went to Ningpo. Having got there, however, he could not find a new religion. No one seemed to have heard of it. For several weeks he lived in the city, earning his living by cutting grass and selling it to people who had cattle to feed, always hoping to hear of the religion that would bring him peace of heart. It was not until the Monday when he encountered Wang the basket-maker that he found it.

Wang the basket-maker was sitting in a tea-shop, talking eagerly to a group of men who were in there sipping tea. He was talking about a God whom he called Jesus, who could forgive sins, when Wang the farmer came in and sat down. However indifferent the other listeners may have been to the preacher's message, one at least was spellbound. Oblivious to the buzz of conversation that came from the men who lounged in bamboo chairs around the little tables of the tea-shop, deaf to the cries of the street vendors and the coolies passing up and down the narrow street outside. Wang the farmer had ears only for what the man at the next table was so eagerly telling those who were sitting with him. Forgiveness of sins, and a free entry into heaven for all who came to this God, Jesus—was not this the new religion that would bring him peace of heart?

Wang the basket-maker and Wang the farmer left the tea-shop together. They spent the evening poring over the New Testament, and Wang the farmer was told that he must go to the Jesus Hall, where the foreign teacher would explain to him still more concerning this Jesus religion. Wang the basket-maker went to bed that night with the knowledge that he had done an important thing.

He found a new job early on Tuesday morning. The very first basket-maker to whom he applied took him on without hesitation. Wang soon discovered the reason for this sudden reversal of fortune. His former employer, angered by his refusal to work on Sundays, had notified all the other basket-makers, who belonged to the same society as himself, not to employ Wang if he came round on Monday looking for work. On Monday, therefore, Wang had hunted in vain. Now it was Tuesday, not Monday, and that was quite a different matter. It was the busy season, Wang was a good basket-maker, and whatever his former employer had meant, he had certainly only said Monday. Any of the men who had turned Wang away the previous day, would willingly have taken him on Tuesday.

It was not long after Hudson had been introduced to Wang the farmer that Wang the basket-maker arrived one day at the Jesus Hall with another man. This time it was a painter, whom he had met in the courtyard of a wealthy family where he had gone to sell baskets. The ladies of the house, standing around him on their tiny, bound feet, wanting little baskets to keep their incense in, had inquired with some annoyance why he refused to make them. The single-hearted Wang explained that as a believer in Jesus, the true God, he could have nothing to do with idols, the incense that was burned to them, nor yet the baskets in which the incense was kept. The ladies had listened to his strange Jesus doctrine for a while, then, tiring of it, had turned back into the house. He was gathering up his baskets to carry them off the premises when a young man, dressed in coolie clothes, suddenly appeared before him.

"What was that you were saying?" demanded the stranger. "You didn't see me. I was up there, painting." He pointed to a ladder that leaned against the wall, under a brightly-colored overhanging roof. "What was it you were saying? I heard—but tell me again."

Wang needed no second bidding. The painter listened again to this surprising news of a living God who wanted to save, not to punish, sinful men, and when it was suggested that he should go to the Jesus Hall to learn more, he readily agreed.

Hudson smiled and bowed at the new arrival. Wang the basket-maker was certainly a good fisher of men. It was only a short time ago that he had brought along Wang the farmer, and now this one. He looked into the dark, earnest eyes of the young working man before him, and asked politely, "What is your honorable surname?"

"My despicable surname," came the answer, "is Wang."

13
READY FOR LAUNCH

Wang the painter shuffled along the narrow passage of No. 1, Beaumont Street, Whitechapel, and opened the front door. In his loose-fitting Chinese clothes, his skimpy pigtail dangling down his back, he looked strangely out of place against the background of a rather dingy little house in a London side-street, and the young man standing outside the door suppressed a start of surprise when he saw him. It had not occurred to him that the missionary from China whom he had come to see would have brought a Chinese servant back with him.

"Is Mr. Taylor at home?" asked young Meadows.

"Please come in," said Wang in his soft, pidgin English. "I go see master," and in a minute he returned to show the visitor into a small, sparsely furnished room. Hudson was sitting there, absorbed in the project that had occupied him since he had returned from China a few months previously. It was a long way from finished—the revision of the New Testament in Chinese.

His pigtail had gone, now that he was back in England, and in his old, well-worn suit he looked like a poor clerk who could not afford to keep a good fire burning in the grate. Cold though the day was, there were only small flames in the fireplace. Young Meadows' quick eyes took in the apparent poverty of the man he had come to see, and who was standing up now, with a welcoming smile on his face, to greet him. When he sat down to a simple dinner with

Hudson and Maria, he observed that the tablecloth had seen better days, and the food, cooked by Wang, was not up to standard. Although he missed none of these facts, he was not discouraged by what he saw of the life of missionaries. These two young people, both under thirty, told him such tense and thrilling stories of besieged cities, escapes from pirates, and wonderful answers to their prayers. He was deeply impressed by their stories and their purpose in life.

It did not matter to them if their clothes were old-fashioned or their carpets had holes. They simply were not concerned about clothes and carpets. What absorbed them was the realization that millions of Chinese knew nothing about the true God, and therefore they must be told. Young Meadows felt the same way about it, and wanting to go to China as soon as possible, decided that Hudson was the missionary society he would like to join.

Hudson had to explain that although he was eager for people to go to China to spread the gospel, and he hoped to return there himself soon, he was not a missionary society, as he had no money. He couldn't send even one missionary to China. Actually, since he had returned to England, a very sick man, he had rarely known from where next month's rent would come. He had long since left the Chinese Evangelization Society, and was so busy completing his medical training and revising the Chinese New Testament that he had no time to "earn a living." It was remarkable how the money came in, sometimes in the very nick of time, from friends and relatives who were interested in him, and in China. He realized that it was God who moved them to do it, and his faith in his heavenly Father increased greatly. All the same, he felt he was in no position to employ missionaries, and said so.

Mr. Meadows, however, felt otherwise. After all, if God could move people to support his servant, Hudson Taylor, could he not also move people to support his servant, Meadows? At any rate, inspired by what he had seen and heard, he assured Hudson that he was willing to go to China on the assumption that God would.

So Hudson obtained his first missionary, who sailed for China a few months later. Remembering his own early experiences in Shanghai, Hudson determined that his missionary should receive money and letters regularly, not spasmodically. He bought a large, important-looking account book, in which he made careful entries of gifts received and transmitted the funds to Mr. Meadows very promptly. He also bought a file to keep letters in, and wrote often. After a year, young Meadows' only cause for complaint was that he was so well looked after, and received money so regularly, that he sometimes felt he was not living by faith in God at all. He seemed quite disappointed at not suffering hardship through shortage of money. Hudson replied that he had no idea where his next month's salary was coming from, or how much it would be, and that they must continue praying to God for supplies. Meadows was reassured.

Still, what was one more missionary in a land where millions upon millions of people were living and dying without once hearing of the only true God? There was a large map of China hanging on the wall of the little study on Beaumont Street, and Hudson's eyes constantly roamed over it as he lifted them from the Chinese and English Bibles on the desk before him. He read over and over again the names of provinces far away from the coast. Such musical, picturesque names stirred his imagination—South of the Clouds, Four Streams, West of the Mountains, North of the Lake, Clear Sea, South of the River. Protestant missionaries had never penetrated into those distant places, and Hudson thought of the hundreds of cities, the thousands of towns, and the tens of thousands of villages they contained. Hundreds, thousands, millions. It was the thought of the millions that continually oppressed him.

Millions of Chinese people—lovable, erring Chinese people, like Mr. Nee, and Wang the basket-maker, and the farmer from the village of O-Zi. He remembered the Chinese people every day as he looked into the face of the faithful painter Wang, who had left home and country to serve him. He remembered the monk who was walled into a cell in the temple, hoping to find "the Way." He thought of Mr. Nee's father, who had sought "the Way" for twenty years, and died without finding it. The more he prayed that God would send missionaries to those far-away provinces, the more he felt he ought to do something about it himself.

He had already approached all the missionary societies he could think of, to urge them to send men to inland China—to those vast provinces with the picturesque names, where millions of people were still waiting to hear of Jesus. He had been listened to sympathetically enough, but told that nothing could be done at present.

The thought came again and again that he ought to start a missionary society himself; one that would go to those remote inland regions—West of the Mountains, South of the Clouds, North of the Lake. He studied the map on his study wall long and earnestly and often. There were eleven great provinces, and the mysterious country of Tibet, with no missionaries.

If only, thought Hudson, there were two missionaries to each province. That would, at any rate, be a start.

And then a much more frightening thought came to his mind. One he did not like at all.

"Then why don't you ask God to send them to you?"

Hudson did not want to start a missionary society to go to inland China. He was quite prepared to go there himself, but he did not want to send other people. Supposing when the young men and women sent by him got there, insufficient money was received to support them? Supposing they died of starvation? Supposing the Chinese were angry at people coming to preach a different religion, and killed them? All sorts of horrible possibilities came to his mind. How terrible, thought Hudson desperately, to have been the one to send them to their death. The responsibility was too great, he felt, and he tried to put away the thought of starting a missionary society. But he could not. There it was, and there it remained.

One Sunday morning in June, on the beach at Brighton, he finally concluded he would have to do it. Walking slowly over the pebbles down to the water's edge, he looked across the calm, sunlit sea with his mind in a turmoil.

Imagine being responsible for sending men and women to the far-off unknown regions of inland China, where they might die of starvation. On the other hand, could he leave those millions of Chinese to die without knowing of God? That was far more dreadful. Suddenly he saw that even if the missionaries did all die of starvation, they would go straight to heaven—and couldn't be better off. If, before they died, they had turned only one Chinese from worshipping the devil to worshipping God, it would have been worth it. This somewhat pessimistic reflection, strangely enough, made him feel quite hopeful.

Then another thought occurred to him. If he did start a missionary society to go to the inland of China, it would only be because he knew that God was urging him to do it. If God was urging him to do it, then all the responsibility for what happened would be God's, not his.

Now why, thought Hudson, had that not occurred to him before? God would be responsible, not he! As this realization sank into his mind, he felt as though a great, crushing load was being gently rolled away.

"Oh, Lord," he prayed with a tremendous sense of relief. "Thou shalt have all the burden!" It had gone already—no longer was he oppressed by the thought of starving missionaries. "I will go forward as thy servant, at thy bidding."

Yes, he must start a missionary society, and now he knew he could. All fears of what might happen in the future had dissolved like a morning mist before the sun. What happened as a result of obeying God's voice was not his responsibility. All he had to do was to go forward, asking God to send what was necessary to start a missionary society to go West of the Mountains, South of the Clouds, North of the Lake.

Eleven provinces and Tibet, thought Hudson. There should be two workers for each, to begin to take the good news of God's love to man to the interior of China. Two times twelve are twenty-four. So Hudson, standing bareheaded on the beach that Sunday morning, closed his eyes. He stood like that for several minutes, the waves lapping at his feet. Then he opened his Bible, and made a note in it. "Prayed for twenty-four willing skillful labourers at Brighton, June 25, 1865." He walked lightheartedly over the pebbles to the promenade where ladies in full skirts strolled with top-hatted gentlemen, and horses trotted between the shafts of coaches and pony traps. He paid little attention to the fashionably-dressed people thronging the seafront. His thoughts were very far away. Twenty-four workers, as well as Maria and himself, to take the good news to the millions in Four Streams, South of the River, Clear Sea, North of the Lake.

He never doubted that God would answer his prayer. Nor did it trouble him that he, who had barely enough money to support his wife, would now begin to require an income of thousands of pounds a year to support the twenty-four willing, skillful laborers. If he was doing God's work in God's way, God would certainly supply all that was required.

Hudson was very practical. The workers and the money

would be provided, were probably already on the way. He must prepare for them. He returned to London on Monday, and on Tuesday he paid a visit to the bank.

"I want to open a new banking account," he told the manager.

"How much have you to start with?" inquired that official.

"Ten pounds."

"And whose name is the banking account to be in?"

"The China Inland Mission," said Hudson, and the missionary society was launched.

14
DESTINATION—INLAND CHINA

Hudson walked along a broad street in the West End, near Regent's Park, and climbing the wide steps of one of the large houses, rang the bell. The door was opened almost immediately by a man servant, and feeling a bit shy, Hudson entered a beautifully furnished hall, very different in appearance to the narrow passage that welcomed his visitors at home.

"Her ladyship is expecting you," he was informed, as he handed the butler his hat and stick. He was then shown into the room where he was to take breakfast with the Dowager Lady Radstock.

It was less than a week since the launching of the China Inland Mission, and Hudson was scarcely prepared for the direction in which things were moving. He was not accustomed to these circles of high society. But his hostess, whom he had met for the first time at church the day before, put him entirely at his ease. She wanted to hear about China, and as he told of those millions in the inland provinces and how God was urging him to go to them, not only she but several others at the breakfast table were interested.

In a surprisingly short time he was receiving invitations to attend luncheon parties with titled people, and to speak at drawing-room meetings where all the guests appeared in evening dress. As the weeks sped by, he found himself carried along as though by a full tide, traveling not only in England, but in Scotland and Ireland, too, to meet people who had heard about his enterprise, and to speak at meetings, large and small.

At one of those meetings he met a bright and witty young man who was later to become the founder of the well-known Dr. Barnardo's Homes. At that time Tom Barnardo was only twenty, and a member of the theological class to which Hudson had been invited to speak. Not being very big himself, when Tom Barnardo saw how short and slight the missionary from China appeared beside the tall, well-built figure of the class leader, he whispered to his neighbor,

"Good! There's a chance for me." For he wanted to go to China, and approached Hudson about joining the Inland Mission. Following Hudson's advice, he took medical training at the London Hospital. There he discovered that his vocation was to rescue waifs and strays in England.

Barnardo was not the only young person stirred into action on hearing of the needs of the Chinese people West of the Mountains, North of the Lake, South of the Clouds. Hudson had prayed for twenty-four skillful, willing workers on that memorable Sunday morning on the Brighton beach, and God was answering that prayer.

The days were never long enough for Hudson now. Traveling, speaking at meetings, interviewing people who wanted to join the mission, writing booklets about China, he went from one task to another with never a stop, it seemed. There were seven or eight missionaries already in China, including Meadows, who were eager to join the mission that was to go to the inland provinces.

As 1866 dawned it became evident that his twenty-four workers had already been given—for sixteen young men and women were prepared to sail with him and Maria to China as soon as arrangements could be made.

The arrangements that needed to be made, of course, all

seemed to require money. Hudson figured that it would cost nearly £2,000 to get him and his party to China, and by the first week in February he had only £170 in hand. They hoped to sail in May. It did not appear very likely that they would, in the circumstances. Somehow Hudson felt sure that God was going to send them all that was required. He and Maria decided they would hold a prayer meeting in their house every day at twelve o'clock, to ask God to do so, and to pray for his direction and help in all connected with their going to China. Once more Hudson proved how very practical it is to pray.

Within five weeks of starting that daily prayer meeting, all the money they needed had come in. One man alone had given £650. All that remained was to find a sailing ship on which the whole party of eighteen adults and four children could be accommodated.

That was not so easy, it seemed. April passed into May, and still no suitable sailing ship bound for China was procurable. Nevertheless—Hudson and his party were still hoping to sail in May.

On May 2nd, Hudson was in Hertfordshire, staying in the home of a Colonel Puget, who had invited him to speak at a meeting about his work. It was what is known as a "good meeting." The audience listened so earnestly and quietly, that the proverbial pin might have been heard to drop. Colonel Puget, the chairman, felt it was too good an opportunity to let pass. Hudson always stipulated that there should be no collection taken up at any of his meetings, but Colonel Puget felt this meeting should be an exception. Why, the people were obviously deeply moved—undoubtedly they would give generously if the plate were passed around. He was a little put out, when Hudson restrained him as he was about to announce that there would be a collection.

"You made a great mistake, if I may say so," he said at supper. "The people were really interested. We might have had a good collection." Although he did not say so, he himself had intended putting £5 in the plate. This enthusiastic young missionary leader was too impractical. His ideal of only asking God for money was splendid, but to refuse to allow a collection at a meeting where people were obviously eager to give was carrying things too far. Colonel Puget retired to bed shaking his head with such thoughts.

Strangely, he could not sleep. As he lay in bed, turning from one side to the other, his thoughts went back to the meeting. Hudson had spoken about the Chinese who were dying without once having heard of the only One who could save them.

"Every hour a thousand of them die, going out into the darkness of an eternity without Christ." Every hour a thousand. . . every hour a thousand. . .The thought of it seemed to burn into the very heart of the good colonel. All thought of the wasted opportunity of taking up a large collection was gone, as he seemed to see the broad stream of Chinese going steadily, hopelessly into the darkness. Something must be done to let them hear about a savior! Something was being done, of course. That gallant little band of laborers. Only young men and women, most of them, prepared to sacrifice their lives if need be, to follow young Hudson Taylor right into the heart of that great eastern empire.

"But what can I do?" thought the elderly colonel, and his thought became a prayer. "Lord," he prayed earnestly, "what wilt thou have me to do?"

He remembered the £5 note he had intended to put in the plate as a donation, and somehow it seemed pathetically small. In the darkness the Colonel prayed again. "Lord, what wilt thou have me to do?" After a long time he fell asleep—but not before he knew what he must do.

The following morning, before the colonel came down to

breakfast, the postman had delivered a letter to Hudson from a firm of shipping agents. A ship called the *Lammermuir* was about to sail for China, and Hudson was offered the entire cabin accommodation for his party. It sounded perfect—but would the price be beyond their reach?

The colonel appeared, explaining that he had had a bad night, and apologizing for being late, and they sat down to breakfast. When it was over, the colonel asked Hudson into his study.

"I have some money here for you," he said, handing him several contributions that had been given him to pass on to Hudson. Then he continued:

"I felt yesterday evening that you were wrong about the collection, but now I see things differently. Lying awake in the night, I thought of that stream of souls in China, a thousand every hour going out into the dark. I could only cry, 'Lord, what wilt thou have me to do?' I think I have his answer," and he handed Hudson a check. "If there had been a collection I should have given a £5 note," he added. "This check is the result of no small part of the night spent in prayer."

Hudson looked in wonderment at the slip of paper in his hand. The check was made out, not for £5, but for £500.

There was no question now as to whether he could afford to book the entire cabin accommodation of the *Lammermuir*. The unexpected check, coming right on the heels of the notification of the sailing vessel seemed to be God's assurance that it was the boat on which he and his party should travel. So, less than a month later, they set sail for China—the first of a steady stream of men and women that for more than eighty years poured in to the great cities and numberless villages of the regions West of the Mountains, South of the Clouds, North of the Lake, to tell men like Mr. Nee, and Wang the basket-maker, and the farmer from O-Zi about Jesus.

*   *   *   *   *

Hudson leaned on the railing of the ship, looking out to sea. It was not yet a year since he had made that entry in his Bible: "Prayed for twenty-four willing skillful labourers at Brighton, June 25, 1865." How quickly things had happened since that day. It seemed as though God had just been waiting for him to take that one step, and when he took it, he found everything else was prepared.

The first time he sailed for China, a lonely young man of twenty, he had only vaguely realized the purpose for which he had been sent. "Go for me to China," the voice had said, and he had obeyed. This time, as a man of thirty-three, he understood more clearly the task that had been set him. He was to lead his little team of workers into the heart of China to spread throughout the length and breadth of that great empire the news of God's love to man.

Difficulties and dangers, hardships and heartaches all lay before him. There was nothing comfortable or easy about the task ahead. This campaign would demand every ounce of his strength and endurance. Nevertheless, he was not afraid. All that was required of him, after all, was loyal obedience to his Master, and unswerving trust in him. Christ was the leader, not he, and with such a leader he was prepared to follow to the end. Hudson leaned on the rails of the *Lammermuir* with an eager, happy heart as she plowed her way through the waters, towards his lifework.

"I heard the call, Come follow,
That was all.

Earth's joys grew dim, My soul went after him.
I rose and followed—that was all.
Will you not follow if you hear him call?"

15
MISSION ACCOMPLISHED

It was forty years after the day on Brighton beach when he had finally decided to found the China Inland Mission, and Hudson was sitting in a mission station in South of the Lake. It was the last of the eleven provinces that had opened to his missionaries. Four Streams, North of the Lake, South of the River, West of the Mountains, South of the Cloud—one by one mission stations had been occupied in all of those inland provinces, but still the hostile officials of thickly populated South of the Lake refused to allow the Westerners with their religion of Jesus to settle there. For over thirty years Hudson had prayed for the door to open, and now at last, even in South of the Lake, the China Inland Mission had its workers.

Hudson looked out of the window across the roofs of the city to the distant horizon. It was his very last day on earth, although no one knew it yet. He did not know it himself. He was thinking more of the past than the future as he turned to talk to his companion.

"It is a wonderful privilege we have, to be able to bring everything to God in prayer, isn't it?" he said with a smile. This was one of the things that impressed him most. God had done so many of the things he had asked him to do. Answering his prayer for twenty-four workers had only been one of them. Hudson had gone on praying for more missionaries, and God had gone on sending them. Only twenty years ago he had prayed for seventy more, and God had sent them. Then, a few years later, he had prayed for another 100, and God had sent them, too. Now there were more than 800 members in the mission, scattered over the whole vast interior of China, in which not one province remained where Jesus was not preached. Many were the obstacles that had been encountered, yet sooner or later they had been overcome. Even now there were difficulties—there always would be—but Hudson knew that as he prayed, God would solve them all.

"A wonderful privilege—to be able to bring everything to God in prayer," he said again.

"Yes. . . " The younger man looked across at the old missionary, and said slowly:

"You know, I sometimes feel I can't bring everything to God. The big things—yes. But many things seem too small to pray to God about. The feeling that they are too small really hinders me from praying."

The elderly Hudson seemed almost surprised. "I don't know anything about that," he said. Too small to pray about? Some of the very small things in his life had led to very big things. Half a crown was not very much money, but giving away the last one he had, over fifty years ago, had started him on the path of faith and obedience. The prick of a pin was small that he scarcely noticed it, yet it had almost cost him his life. A pigtail was really a very small thing—yet how large it had loomed when he was the first and only missionary to wear one. One of the shortest prayers of his life had been when he prayed on the beach, but it had started the mission for inland China. Who could say what was big and what was not?

"There is nothing small, and there is nothing great," he said, after a slight pause. "Only God is great." Then, as though summing up all the experience of the years, he added simply, "We should trust him fully."

He went to bed very soon after that, for he was tired. It had been a happy day. In the morning he had gone to the chapel to speak to the Chinese Christians—men and women of South of the Lake, who had found "the Way." That afternoon he had had tea on the little lawn in the garden, and met all the other missionaries in the city, who had come to visit him. He had enjoyed it all very much, but now he was tired, and thought he would not go downstairs for supper.

"We'll bring it up to you in bed," he was told, and he went into his room. Twilight fell over the city. The outline of the distant mountains faded into the darkness, and in the sky overhead the stars appeared. It was very quiet. After a time light footsteps were heard on the stairs, as the supper tray was carried up. The door of Hudson's room was opened, then there was silence again, followed by quickly running footsteps and a cry from the top of the stairs.

"Doctor! Doctor!" He came immediately, but as soon as he looked at the happy, peaceful face on the pillow, he knew he was not needed.

*　　*　　*　　*　　*

"Venerable Pastor, Venerable Pastor," whispered the young evangelist, bending over the quiet form on the bed, holding one of the cold hands in his two warm ones. He had come in from an outstation that very day, in order to see the famous old missionary of whom he had heard so much. And now he must speak to him, even though his words would not be heard.

"Venerable Pastor, we truly love you. We have come today to see you. We longed to look into your face. We, too, are your little children—Venerable Pastor, Venerable Pastor. You opened for us the road, the road to heaven. You loved us and prayed for us long years. We came today to look upon your face.

"You look so happy, so peaceful! You are smiling. Your face is quiet and pleased. You cannot speak to us tonight. We do not want to bring you back; but we will follow you. We shall come to you, Venerable Pastor. You will welcome us by and by."

Hudson had been welcomed already. As one of the Chinese women said as she looked at him, her eyes full of tears, but a smile on her face. "Ten thousand times ten thousands of angels have received him!" Above their welcome rang one voice he had learned to listen for on earth. The One he loved beyond all others, and had once said, "Go for me to China." But this time the voice said, "Well done! Good, faithful servant! Enter into the joy of thy Lord!"